Advance praise for *The Gifts of Near-Death Experiences*

The Gifts of Near Death Experiences: You Don't Have to Die to Experience Your True Home brings a fresh and exciting perspective to understanding near-death experiences. *Everyone* can benefit from learning the wisdom so clearly and eloquently expressed in this book. With each turn of the page you will find a treasure trove of insights, inspiration, and practical pointers that will *really* work in your life. This outstanding book is expertly written, remarkably easy to read, and enthusiastically recommended.

> —Jeffrey Long, M. D., author of the *New York Times* bestselling *Evidence of the Afterlife: The Science of Near-Death Experiences*

"The Linns have written a book that is both inspirational and practical. They provide wise and gentle wisdom that lead readers into a place of growth and healing."

> —Richard Rohr O. F. M, author of *Falling Upward*

"*The Gifts of Near-Death Experiences* will help you develop your own spiritual practice of meditation that can crack open your inner-door so that you too may glimpse beyond into Infinite Love and Light and live a life of love."

> —Peter Panagore, author of *Heaven is Beautiful*

An extraordinary accomplishment! Yes, *The Gifts of Near-Death Experiences* is filled with gripping stories, verified research, and more than enough supportive material to stop you in your tracks. Yet there's more. Much more. The authors, Sheila Fabricant, Dennis and Matthew Linn, all three experienced, globe-trotting teachers and counselors, have put together thoughts, suggestions, and how-tos at the end of each chapter to enable YOU the reader to feel what is revealed and then take it into your own life, be one with it, live it NOW (not next week). In fact, everything in this book, no matter the subject, is available, usable. I love the "now-ness" of this, the alive-ness. You don't have to die to experience the truth about yourself, where you're from or where you're going once you leave this life behind. Surprise. . .this is not a book about near-death, not really, it is a book about YOU, the real YOU."

—P. M. H. Atwater, L. H. D., researcher of near-death states, author of such books as *Near-Death Experiences: The Rest of the Story, Future Memory, Dying to Know You: Proof of God in the Near-Death Experience*, and *Children of the Fifth World*.

THE GIFTS OF
NEAR-DEATH
EXPERIENCES

THE GIFTS OF NEAR-DEATH EXPERIENCES

You Don't Have to Die
to Experience Your True Home

Dennis Linn
Sheila Fabricant Linn
Matthew Linn

HAMPTON ROADS

Cover design by Jim Warner
Cover art © Pellinni | Dreamstime.com
Interior designed by Howie Severson

Hampton Roads Publishing Company, Inc.
Charlottesville, VA 22906
Distributed by Red Wheel/Weiser, LLC
www.redwheelweiser.com
Sign up for our newsletter and special offers by going to
www.redwheelweiser.com/newsletter/.

ISBN: 978-1-57174-743-3

Library of Congress Cataloging-in-Publication Data
Names: Linn, Dennis, author.
Title: The gifts of near-death experiences : you don't have to die to experience
  your true home / Dennis Linn, Sheila Fabricant Linn, Matthew Linn.
Description: Newburyport : Hampton Roads Pub., 2016. | Includes
  bibliographical references.
Identifiers: LCCN 2015050623 | ISBN 9781571747433 (6 x 9 tp : alk. paper)
Subjects: LCSH: Near-death experiences.
Classification: LCC BF1045.N4 L56 2016 | DDC 133.901/3--dc23
LC record available at http://lccn.loc.gov/2015050623

Printed in Canada
MAR
10 9 8 7 6 5 4 3 2 1

Dedicated to Zeke Pierce
and his beloved parents, brothers, and sister
Crawford, Liv, Max, Mia, and Nikken

Contents

Foreword

KENNETH RING, PH.D.
Professor Emeritus of Psychology
University of Connecticut

On May 21, 2012, I received an intriguing email from a trio of authors in Colorado, which contained a rare compliment: they were planning to write a book modeled after one of mine dealing with near-death experiences, *Lessons from the Light.* They wanted to advise me of their intent to make sure it was okay with me. They also asked if I might be willing to confer with them about their undertaking.

I had not heard of these authors, but apparently many others had. I learned that they—a husband and wife, and the brother of the husband—specialized in giving retreats and seminars on spirituality and healing, that they had done so in about sixty countries, and had already written some twenty-two books, which collectively had sold over a million copies. These were certainly well-established and successful authors, so I quickly assented, and with delight, to their overture.

This was the beginning of what has become a deep and loving friendship with the Linns—Denny and Sheila, Denny's brother Matt, and John, Denny and Sheila's teenage son. But that is another story. First, I need to say a bit about the book you are now about to read.

Actually, I should preface this with just a word about *Lessons from the Light*. The main idea of that book was that if readers really absorbed the implications of the research on near-death experiences (NDEs), they could reap many of the benefits that near-death experiencers themselves gained from their encounter with death. In that context, I argued that such an immersion in this material might function rather like what I called "a benign virus"; that is, by exposing themselves to the world of NDEs, readers could "catch it."

The Linns wanted to do something similar in their book, but really develop this idea, take it deeper, and do it in a much more systematic way than I had. Indeed, once they had read my book, they realized that rather like Monsieur Jourdan in Molière's play, *Le Bourgeois gentilhomme*, who was shocked to learn that he had been speaking prose all his life, they had long been speaking the language of NDEs. In short, they had already been offering a very similar perspective in their retreats and writing.

And this aim has been ably achieved in *The Gifts of Near-Death Experiences*. Of course, in the two score and more years since the publication of Raymond Moody's groundbreaking best seller, *Life After Life*, which introduced the world to the concept of near-death experiences, there have been many books on the subject, often written by NDErs themselves. These have thrilled and inspired millions of people. But there have been very few books that have attempted to distill the findings of NDE narratives and research so that readers who have not had an NDE themselves could learn how they, too, could come to see the world and live their lives as NDErs do.

The Gifts of Near-Death Experiences does this superbly, better than any book I know. So, although it, too, is replete with inspiring stories of NDEs, it is primarily a book with a *practical* focus. Every chapter ends with processes, so that the reader can apply the lessons of that chapter in his or her own life. Thus, you will be taken through all the major features of an NDE, and then you will be helped, if you choose, to absorb their benefits into your own life.

Ah, but there is so much more to this book than this bare summary would suggest because it's not just about NDEs; it's also about the role of NDEs and their implications in the lives of the Linns themselves. They offer the reader many intimate glimpses into their own personal history, their daily life, and their life in their community in such a way as to enable you to see just how they have been able to apply the lessons of the NDE in their own lives. Many of these vignettes reveal just how thoughtfully they themselves have been able to practice what they preach (though they *never* preach—they only invite). None of them has ever had an NDE as such, but they certainly show the effects of having caught "the benign virus." The hoary expression of "walking your talk" certainly applies to these authors.

I have been lucky enough to see this for myself. After many delightful email exchanges, they suggested that, inasmuch as I was planning to visit one of my daughters in Colorado, I might want to spend some time with them during which I could actively collaborate with them on their book over a period of several days. I accepted with alacrity.

Once my visit to my daughter was over with, a friend of the Linns drove me to their house in the Colorado mountains. There were fifty-five steps up a seemingly small mountain to their front door—for a moment, I thought I was back in Amsterdam! But the Linns were very welcoming, and we all had a wonderful and warm conversation over the dinner that Sheila had gone to a great deal of trouble to prepare.

But trouble of another kind was soon to come.

In the morning, after taking a shower, I nearly burned down their house.

When the shower was over, I turned on the switch that controlled the heat lamp in their downstairs bathroom. Or I had innocently assumed that it did. I was wrong.

It actually controlled the sauna in the adjacent room.

That sauna was used only for storage.

Soon smoke began to billow out, the smoke alarms went off, and all hell broke loose!

Matt, who had been sleeping in the room next to mine, jumped out into the hallway, the other Linns, who had been sleeping upstairs, leapt out of their beds and came charging downstairs (Denny injuring his leg in the process), and we all began furiously trying to beat out the fire before it spread any further.

It was touch and go for several minutes, but finally it was quelled.

I felt like killing myself.

By now, the fire brigade had arrived—the paramedics, ambulances, the works. We all had to clear out for a time.

When we were allowed back in, the house reeked of smoke, although the actual structural damage was confined mostly to the sauna.

The rest of the day was devoted to various officials coming by—insurance inspectors, cleaning people, etc.

The house would be uninhabitable for several days. (Fortunately, there was an attached house that was empty that we could use in the meantime.)

So much for our book collaboration!

By now, I had learned that though the Linns had insurance, their deductible was still $5,000. I wanted to pay them before killing myself.

And you know what? They wouldn't hear of it! I insisted, they resisted. I persisted. Finally, Sheila told me in so many words that she would whack me if I dared even mention the subject again.

I won't continue with everything that took place over the next few days except to say that all the Linns did was to offer me love, support, kisses, and promises of their enduring friendship. We had the best time together—despite everything—and shared many intimate personal stories. We even managed to get quite a lot of work done on their book.

This is how I really came to know and love the Linns. That's the kind of people they are.

They will probably object to the way this foreword has ended, since they are very modest and self-effacing. But, hell, although this is their book, it is my foreword, and I'll write it the way I want!

However, I only mention all this to make it clear to you that under the most frightening and stressful of circumstances, the Linns showed me just how much they already were the perfect ones to write the book you now hold in your hands.

I also learned to take showers in dim light, if necessary.

Acknowledgments

We wish to gratefully acknowledge the following people for their kindness and care in helping us with the manuscript for this book: Margaret Grant, Barbara Harris Whitfield, Michael Imperi, Julie Keith, Kenneth Ring, Frances Shure, Bert Thelen, and Zeke's Family.

We also wish to express our appreciation to Greg Brandenburgh and his colleagues at Hampton Roads: You are a joy to work with!

Introduction: Catching the Benign Virus

There is a six-hour stretch of road between my home in Colorado and Santa Fe, New Mexico, that I (Denny) have traveled at least fifty times. I thoroughly enjoy it, because the road is full of memories. It passes by some of the snow-capped "fourteeners" (mountains over fourteen thousand feet high) that I have climbed with my family, the streams we have rafted, and the lakes we have fished. I have been there so many times that I know what will be around the next curve in the road.

What surprises us is that people who have had near-death experiences (NDErs) often report something similar. Not only do they see mountains, streams, and lakes, but even more remarkable, they remember having been there before, to the point that they know what will be around the next curve.

For example, following is the near-death experience of Arthur Yensen, who was in a car accident:

> Gradually the earth scene faded away, and through it loomed a bright, new, beautiful world—beautiful beyond imagination! . . .
>
> In the background were two beautiful, round-topped mountains, similar to Fujiyama in Japan. The tops were snow-capped, and the slopes were adorned with foliage of indescribable beauty. The mountains appeared to be about fifteen miles away, yet I could see individual flowers growing on their slopes. I estimated my vision to be about one hundred times better than on earth.

To the left was a shimmering lake containing a different kind of water—clear, golden, radiant, and alluring. It seemed to be alive. The whole landscape was carpeted with grass so vivid, clear, and green, that it defies description. To the right was a grove of large, luxuriant trees, composed of the same clear material that seemed to make up everything.

. . . Then I noticed that the landscape was gradually becoming familiar. It seemed as if I had been here before. I remembered what was on the other side of the mountains. Then with a sudden burst of joy, I realized that this was my real home! Back on earth I had been a visitor, a misfit, and a homesick stranger. With a sigh of relief I said to myself, Thank God I'm back again. This time I'll stay![1]

Why Do Near-Death Experiences Fascinate Us?

Raymond Moody first used the term *near-death experience*. He was referring to experiences like Arthur's, in which people appear to be dead or dying, leave their bodies, find themselves fully conscious in another realm, and then return to this life. Since the 1975 publication of Moody's book, *Life After Life*,[2] accounts of near-death experiences (NDEs) have been widely disseminated and are fascinating to a broad spectrum of the population worldwide. They have captured the public imagination in a profound way. For example, we notice that whenever NDEs come up in our conversations with a wide range of people, they appear fascinated and eager to learn more. Why?

I wonder if the reason for this profound attraction to NDEs is that hearing about them triggers a memory deep within us. It is sort of like a homecoming. Accounts of NDEs are like echoes that resonate from somewhere inside ourselves so that we want to keep hearing stories that awaken us more fully to that awareness.

—Raymond Moody, The Light Beyond[3]

Near-Death Experiences, Shared-Death Experiences, and the Like

What actually happens during a near-death experience? Dr. Jeffrey Long and his wife, Jody, have the largest collection of NDE accounts in the world that is publicly accessible. As of now, they have over four thousand accounts of NDEs in more than twenty languages.[4] They find that, in general, the same basic elements occur all over the world:

> Whether it's a near-death experience of a Hindu in India, a Muslim in Egypt, or a Christian in the United States, the same core elements are present in all, including out-of-body experience, tunnel experience, feelings of peace, beings of light, a life review, reluctance to return, and transformation after the NDE. In short, the experience of dying appears similar among all humans, no matter where they live.
>
> . . . Near-death experiences remind us that although the people on Earth may be a world apart, they may share this important spiritual experience. It's amazing to think that no matter what country we call home, perhaps our real home is in the wondrous unearthly realm consistently described by NDErs around the world.[5]

Because they transcend religious affiliation and culture, Kenneth Ring calls NDEs the "universal donor."

In "shared death experiences" (SDEs), loved ones or other caregivers accompanying a dying person experience some of the elements listed above, including leaving their bodies, seeing deceased loved ones and beings of Light, sharing in the dying person's life review, and so forth. In other words, they go partway on the journey.

This happened within Raymond Moody's own family. His story is especially convincing because several family members experienced the same thing simultaneously. When Dr. Moody's

mother was dying, he, his wife, his two sisters, and their hus-
bands were by the mother's bedside.

> As we held hands around the bed, the room seemed to change
> shape and four of the six of us felt as though we were being lifted
> off the ground. I had the feeling that the room had turned into the
> shape of an hour-glass. I felt a strong pull, like a riptide that was
> pulling me out to sea, only the pull was upward.
>
> "Look," said my sister, pointing to a spot at the end of the bed.
> "Dad's here! He's come back to get her!"
>
> Everyone there reported later that the light in the room changed to
> a soft and fuzzy texture. It was like looking at light in a swimming
> pool at night.[6]

Later, one of Dr. Moody's brothers-in-law said, "I felt like I
left my physical body and went into another plane with her. It
was like nothing that had ever happened to me."[7]

NDEs have sometimes been dismissed as hallucinations
caused by a drugged and/or dying brain. SDEs indicate that this
could not be the case, since those who have SDEs are typically
healthy people, and more than one healthy person may participate in the same SDE.

The elements of an NDE are not limited to near-death situations, but also occur in more or less healthy people, sometimes
during physical or psychological emergencies but also during
seemingly ordinary moments of life. Such experiences might be
called "Near-Death-Like-Experiences."[8]

Why Now?

When we mention NDEs in conversation or when speaking to
groups, almost everyone knows someone who has had an NDE.
Approximately 12 to 18 percent of people who nearly die have
an NDE; we do not know why some people who are near death

have an NDE and others do not.[9] In a 1992 Gallup poll, the number of people in the United States who have had NDEs was estimated at about fourteen million, or about 5 percent of our population at the time.[10] A more recent study, reported by the International Association for Near-Death Studies, estimates that between 4 and 15 percent of the world's population has had a near-death experience.[11]

People have had NDEs throughout human history; why are we increasingly aware of them now? A partial explanation may be that modern medicine has a greater capacity to resuscitate people, such as those who have cardiac arrests and who might not have recovered several decades ago. This in turn means that more medical staff members have heard stories of NDEs from patients, and they are increasingly open to taking these stories seriously rather than assuming patients are delusional and calling a psychiatrist.

We also find it significant that NDEs and the widespread study of them are so much in our awareness at this present time of a profound shift in human consciousness. The NDE seems to reveal a different way of being in the world that matches this shift. We humans have lived for the past several thousand years believing we are essentially selfish, aggressive, and ultimately on our own, and that we must compete in order to survive. However, research on the frontiers of science, including quantum physics, cellular biology, and epigenetics, is revealing that we are "all connected at the deepest level as one being."[12] This one being is made of infinite, unconditional, and universal love. That is the message of the NDE.

Sometimes, in more extensive NDEs, people realize that they *are* the love and Light they encounter, they are one with everything, they are eternal. NDErs often describe their experience as "more real than life itself," and they are usually profoundly changed by it for the better.[13]

Even the most hardened of criminals and the sickest of sociopaths may return from an NDE ready and able to love others. For example, Caroline Myss shares the following story:

I know one man personally who was a mercenary who was "on his way to work one day," meaning he was off to shoot three people, when he had an accident and had a near-death experience. Suddenly he was out of his body and surrounded by the individuals he had murdered, all of whom told him he had to stop immediately. Needless to say, he did. But let me add, the message was delivered with compassion and not the fires of hell. Today he obviously leads a very different life.[14]

What if we all had an NDE? Could we ever go to war again? Could we ever knowingly hurt another human being or any other living thing, including the Earth itself? What would happen to the problems and hurts that cause so much stress in our lives, such as addictions and compulsions, low self-esteem, grief for the loss of loved ones and fear of death? These are all ways we can get stuck emotionally, and we might say that emotional stuckness is forgetting who we are. An NDE is remembering. In other words, the effects of an NDE are also the symptoms of remembering who we really are . . . of coming home to ourselves.

Coming Back

Many people who have NDEs want to remain in what they recognize as their true home. They do not want to return to a world in which the social environment is so contrary to the realm of light and love they have experienced. The NDEr may struggle to find a safe place to be.

For example, when we are in the Boston area, we usually give a program at the women's prison in Framingham, at the invitation of the chaplain. The first time we went, Ellie, a volunteer in the pastoral care department, accompanied us through security. I (Sheila) felt some fear at all the clanging of keys and banging of steel doors behind us, but Ellie had wonderful energy, and I felt safe with her. I noticed that she was limping. When I asked her why she volunteered at the prison, she told me she had been in a car accident and had had an NDE. Except for her limp, she recovered. She began going to churches, looking for the love she had felt during her NDE. She didn't find it. Then she came to volunteer at the prison. It was with the inmates, she said, that she felt closest to the infinite, unconditional love she had experienced during her NDE.

By the end of the day, I knew what she meant. A cloud of mercy seemed to hang over the whole place. Perhaps the women's vulnerability and lack of persona or pretense—so unlike most of our culture—allow them to resonate to the Light in a way that was palpable to me. In prison, people at least know that what they have been doing doesn't work, and they are reaching out for help. Perhaps their openness makes a way for the loving Light to come and put its arms around the prison. For Ellie, profoundly changed by her NDE, it was the least alien, most nourishing place she could find.

What About the Rest of Us?

The immersion in unconditional love that Ellie experienced and that is so characteristic of NDEs seems to offer a solution to our most serious personal and social problems. How can the rest of us, who have not had an NDE, benefit from this?

The inspiration for this book came from Frances Shure and Dr. Kenneth Ring. Fran is a social activist whose political advocacy includes a particularly controversial issue. She publicly speaks up about this issue in ways that have brought death threats and other forms of retaliation to some of her colleagues. When we asked Fran, "Where do you get your courage?" she said, "It comes from reading about near-death experiences. I've used them for my morning meditation for the past ten years." She showed us her current NDE reading, Lessons from the Light, by Kenneth Ring.[15]

In his book, Ken (now a beloved friend and mentor for this present work) suggests that not only NDErs but all the rest of us, as well, can open ourselves to the lessons of the NDE. He describes the NDE as a "benign virus," by which he means that just getting absorbed in hearing or reading about NDEs, as Fran did, can have some of the same effects upon us as actually having an NDE.[16] We experienced this as we read Ken's book, listened to friends who have had NDEs, and immersed ourselves in more of the NDE literature. It was, for us, a "homecoming," as Moody puts it.

As we read about the elements of an NDE, we realized that most are similar to processes for growth and healing that we have led for many years in our retreats and seminars all over the world. Our experience tells us these are universal processes that are built into us. Thus, in this book we offer the healing processes we have used with our participants, but with a different intention: we offer these processes as avenues or windows into the state of consciousness of people who have actually had an NDE, so that we can enter that same state at least to some degree.

Zeke

The consequences of catching the benign virus of the NDE became all the more evident to us as we were writing this book, when we (Denny and Sheila) had a living experience of its importance. Our son's fifteen-year-old lifelong friend, Zeke, suffered a severe head injury in a mountain bike accident. He never regained consciousness and died five days later. Zeke's family called us to the hospital, and we were with them during most of those five days. Zeke was almost entirely brain-dead, with no activity above the brain stem, and his parents had to decide to take him off life support and let him go.

Even though it had been clear to Zeke's parents from the first moment they saw him in the emergency room that he was no longer in his body, the turning point in their ability to let him go came as they fully grasped the real presence of Zeke's spirit loving them. Signs of this were the dreams Zeke's brother and sister were having, in which Zeke spoke to them and seemed to be guiding medical decisions that needed to be made. At the same time, our own son John sensed Zeke in John's bedroom at home. Zeke also appeared to a close friend of the family in another country and told her, "I'm okay." We encouraged Zeke's family to trust these experiences.

Knowing that he was still present but in another form, the family was able to gather around Zeke's bed and say goodbye to his physical life. We invited each family member to hold his hand or touch his face and in turn tell Zeke what they loved about him and how they wanted him to continue to be with them. Then they could trust that taking him off life support and letting his body go was the best way to have him present everywhere and forever.

After Zeke died, we were responsible for the memorial service at the school he attended with John. The whole community was distraught, with people in various stages of shock and grief. In a much simpler and briefer way, we replicated with the thousand people who attended the service what we had done with Zeke's family in the hospital. Grieving is a process, and each person who loved Zeke is still going through it in his or her own way. However, our awareness of Zeke's ongoing presence and our ability to transmit that to the group did seem to help many people and open them to a world of love and connection that transcends death. We believe it was simply our openness to NDEs and the extent to which we have caught the benign virus by immersing ourselves in them that gave us an intuitive sense of how to be present to Zeke's family in the hospital and to the larger community at the memorial service.

This experience has deepened our awareness of the importance of near-death experiences for both living and dying. We want our readers to catch the benign virus, access the healing and transformative power of the NDE, and become fully alive . . . without having to die.

How to Use This Book

Our goal is for you to catch the benign virus. You can use this book in various ways to help you do so. You can simply read it, notice what moves you, and let that grow inside you. You can also do the healing processes and reflection questions at the end of each chapter. You may wish to watch the videos of NDErs' brief personal accounts that accompany each chapter in this book; if so, see Appendix D and the *The Gifts of Near-Death Experiences* free online video stories seminar on our website, *www.linnministries.org*. You can do any of this on your own, or you may wish to invite one or more companions to join you. Most of all, you can watch and wait for people who have had NDEs themselves and who may sense that your heart is open to them and you will listen.

We do believe you can receive the healing benefits of the near-death experience without having to die. Dr. Jeffrey Long describes how this happened to him:

> *For me personally, I'm showing more love to others now than before I started my near-death experience studies. My understanding of near-death experiences has made me a better doctor. I face life with more courage and confidence. I believe NDErs really do bring back a piece of the afterlife. When NDErs share their remarkable experiences, I believe a piece of the afterlife, in some mysterious way, becomes available to us all.*[17]

⁀ 1 ⁀

Musical Chairs:
Remembering Our Home

We have given seminars in over sixty countries. In places with a long history of war and division, we may have participants from both sides of the conflict. For example, in Northern Ireland we had the families of people who were murdered during the conflict between Protestants and Catholics and the killers in the same room, helping them to forgive one another and reconnect with deceased loved ones.

Participants in our programs also come from a wide variety of classes and social backgrounds. We often work in Mexico, which has a deeply entrenched class system. We know maids in wealthy homes there who have served a family for many years, yet never eaten a meal at the same table as their employers. An aspect of our seminars in Mexico that moves us deeply is when an upper class family and their maid come to the seminar together, sit together, and participate in healing processes together.

With such diverse groups, how can we help people experience their common humanity? We usually begin with a process that we have found especially helpful in this regard. We ask for seven volunteers and invite them up onto the stage, where we have arranged six chairs in a circle. Then we play musical chairs in the usual, competitive way. During each round, as the music plays, the volunteers walk around the circle of chairs. When the music stops, each one tries to sit in a chair. Whoever is left without a chair has to leave the game. Following each round we remove a chair. At the end, one chair is left, with one winner sitting in it.

Then we play a second time with the same people, but we change one of the rules. Following each round we again remove a chair, but the remaining chairs can be shared. By the end of the game, the last chair has seven people piled upon it. Most recently in Mexico, the seven people included Denny and Sheila's son, John, and six adoring señoras. Some of the ladies were servants, and some were their wealthy employers. All of them were laughing and holding on to one another so that no one fell off the chair. Seven winners.[1]

We asked our volunteers and then the entire audience, "Which game did you like better?" The unanimous response was the second one. When we asked them why they preferred the second way of playing, they said that the first way of playing resembled the usual way of living in their culture, based on competition that divides people into winners and losers. The second way was how they want to live, in a world of cooperation where everyone helps each other and everyone wins. They realized that their happiest moments are when they live this way.

We noticed that their comments mirrored the changes so often reported by NDErs. However much their lives prior to their NDE have been consumed by our culture's values of competition, when they return they typically refuse to live that way any longer and often dedicate themselves to cooperation and service. NDErs remember that their original home is a world of loving union, and revisiting that home during their NDE generally affects them so powerfully that they do their best to live that way here. It is as if their energy has been cleansed of the ways our culture has distorted it and has been restored to its original frequency.

Mystical Experiences Change Us Personally and Socially

An NDE is perhaps the most powerful of mystical experiences. Commenting on the transformative power of mystical experiences in general, Aldous Huxley wrote,

> A population trained to make use of such "other kinds of seeing" as the aesthetic, the visionary, and the mystical would be unmanageable by the traditional methods of narcotizing or inebriating propaganda. In the eyes of the politicians and generals who control our destinies, it is most undesirable that the mass of humanity should be trained to see the world as beauty, as mysteriousness, as unity. It is in a culture-conditioned world of utilitarian values, dogmatic bumptiousness, and international dissensions that our rulers have come to the top; and that is the kind of world they would like their subjects to go on being conditioned to create for themselves. Meanwhile let us derive what comfort we may from the thought that other kinds of seeing are always there, parted from the normal waking of consciousness (in William James's words) "by the filmiest of screens."[2]

It is an "other kind of seeing" that significantly inoculates the NDEr against the competitive values of musical chairs #1. Perhaps this is why two of the most common changes following an NDE are increases in a sense of social justice and in the desire to help others.[3]

It also seems significant to us that when hospice patients share their greatest regrets about their lives, the things they most wish they had done match what NDErs report having become most important to them now. For example, the most common regret among hospice patients is, "I wish I'd had the courage to live a life true to myself, not the life others expected of me," followed by "I wish I hadn't worked so hard." NDErs commonly report a new freedom to live as their real self rather than according to the expectations of others, as well as a change in their priorities so that loving relationships are now far more important than work. Thus, it seems that when we are most in touch with our true nature, whether because of an NDE or some other experience that cuts through cultural distortions, we all know what matters most in life.[4]

We were very aware of this recently when we talked with our friend, Ralph. We hadn't seen him since he had an NDE six months before. Ralph had been a driven workaholic, always worried about his business and frantically running from one thing to another, trying to live up to what he believed his culture expected of him. Although he was thinner than when we last saw him and still recovering from the illness that led to his NDE, Ralph's energy or frequency felt entirely different to us. Ralph said that he now had no fear of dying or of living, and that during his NDE, although he no longer had a body, "I was truly and entirely Ralph for the first time." Despite months of illness, he had no worry about his business and knew without doubt that everything would be okay. His need to scramble and win was gone. He spoke of how grateful he was to be with his family, and the love between Ralph, his wife, and their children was palpable. He had a deep peace and stillness so inviting that we wanted to sit next to him forever. We noticed ourselves growing more peaceful in Ralph's presence, as if our own frequencies were aligning themselves with his. As Ken Ring puts it,

> . . . it is not only learning about and absorbing the lessons of the NDE that helps to transmit the benign virus; it can also be "caught" simply by exposing oneself to the energy emitted by the physical presence of NDErs.[5]

NDErs Play Musical Chairs the Second Way

The shift in Ralph's energy is one of many signs that in his life on earth, Ralph has moved from the first way of playing musical chairs to the second. The changes in Ralph are typical of people who have NDEs or near-death-like experiences. These changes, which are often rapid and dramatic, are "strikingly consistent across cultures, races, and creeds," and they "are generally not what would have been expected from pre-existing societal beliefs, religious teachings, or any other source of earthly knowledge."[6] NDErs typically change in the following ways, all of which we observed in Ralph: They grow in love, compassion, and self-esteem. They tend to become more spiritual and less religious; church attendance goes down. They lose all fear of death and have an abiding sense of being loved unconditionally. They realize that all that really matters in life is to love and to learn.[7] (See Appendix C.) Seventy-nine percent of NDErs change significantly; for 19 percent of them, the changes are so profound that they seem like an entirely different person.[8]

We wonder if we might summarize the NDE as an experience of temporarily leaving a world based upon the first way of playing musical chairs and visiting a world based upon the second way. The first way is really a delusion that denies the underlying unity of all things. The second way of playing musical chairs is based upon the truth of who we really are, a truth that becomes evident to the NDEr.

We believe the participants in our seminars recognize this and prefer the second way of playing because it reminds them of who they are and where they come from. Without realizing it until we began reading about NDEs, for as long as we have been giving seminars we have been trying to help people experience, albeit usually in a less dramatic way, what happens during an NDE. Perhaps that is why we resonated so deeply to Ken Ring's book *Lessons from the Light*, and recognized that the processes we have used in our seminars mirror the typical stages of an NDE as he and others describe them. In this book, we will use these processes in the hope that they will help our readers catch the benign virus. As we and our readers catch the virus and experience some of the same changes as NDErs, the rules of musical chairs #1 may become increasingly unsatisfying and even intolerable. We may all find ourselves at home in the world of musical chairs #2.

Positive Memories of Love

After playing both versions of musical chairs with our seminar participants, we ask them to get in touch with a positive memory of a time when they experienced love, union, connection, and cooperation. The reason we do this is to deepen their sense that it is possible to live this way because they have already done so, and to establish a safe and loving environment for the presentations and processes that will follow. Beginning with positive memories parallels the stage of an NDE in which the experiencer is enfolded in peace and love, presumably as preparation for the immensity of what will follow. We turn now to that stage.

⌁ 2 ⌁

Beyond Words:
Ineffability, Peace, and Love

I had heart failure and clinically died. . . . I rose up and I was a few feet up looking down on my body. There I was, with people working on me. I had no fear. No pain. Just peace. . . . There was a sense of perfect peace and contentment; love.[1]

There was an indescribable feeling of love and warmth. It could be like a child before birth in its mother's womb. I felt nothing but peace and tranquility. I never wanted to leave—it was as if I was searching for this place my whole life.[2]

. . . if you took the one thousand best things that ever happened to you in your life and multiplied by a million, maybe you could get close to this feeling. . . . Everything was perfect. . . . I was just an infinite being in perfection. And love and safety and security and knowing that nothing could happen to you and you're home forever. That you're safe forever. And that everybody else was.[3]

This is the hardest thing to try and explain. . . . Words will not come close to capturing the feelings, but I'll try: total, uncondi-tional, all-encompassing love, compassion, peace, warmth, safety, belonging, understanding, overwhelming sense of being home. . . .[4]

In these accounts of NDEs, the experiencer struggles to explain what has happened because human language is impossibly inadequate. Perhaps that is why Raymond Moody's list of the twelve elements of an NDE* begins with "The ineffability of the experience."

Moody describes the second element as "A feeling of peace and quiet; pain is gone." We chose the words "peace" and "love" as the heading of this chapter because they are the two most common words used to describe an NDE and are often used together. These qualities entirely transcend the physical circum-stances, however uncomfortable.

For example, one woman attempted suicide by throw-ing herself into forty-eight-degree ocean water, where she was hurled against rocks. She felt very cold in the ocean and was shivering in the hospital after her NDE. However, in describing her experience, she said,

All of a sudden there was no pain, just peace . . . there's a defi-nite feeling of sunlight and warmth associated with this peaceful feeling . . . when this feeling of peace came over me, I was warm. I felt warm, safe, happy, relaxed, just every wonderful adjective you could use.[5]

---

* Various researchers on near-death experiences have different lists of the elements of an NDE. The order is approximately the same, but the shorter lists may condense some of the elements. See Appendix A.

Thus, the starting point of a near-death experience is peace and love, to an extent that is ineffable—indescribable in human language.

Peace and Love Are the Beginning of Healing

In our books, retreats, and seminars, we always begin by encouraging our audience to recall a moment of peace and love. We explain that when we are in touch with such a moment, we have hope that we can feel this way again. We also are more likely to have the strength and courage to confront the hurts we want to heal.

But really . . . how did the three of us know to do this? Perhaps we (and you) instinctively know that peace and love are our true condition and reflect the fundamental nature of the universe. Perhaps that is why we are all likely to feel at home when we experience these things; they remind us of who we are, and when we remember who we are, we can handle whatever follows.

Peace and Love Transform the Body

After encouraging our readers or retreatants to recall a moment of peace and love, we ask them to hold a feeling of appreciation for that moment in their hearts so that it permeates not only their awareness but their bodies as well. We came to understand the bodily dimension of this when we learned about research at the Institute of HeartMath. This research demonstrates that if you hold a feeling of appreciation for a memory of love in your heart for even just a few seconds, your heart will begin to vibrate at a different frequency.[6] Your heart rhythm will become more coherent (ordered, harmonious, and efficient) rather than incoherent (random and jagged). This affects all other bodily systems.

Since the heart generates the body's most powerful electromagnetic field (about five thousand times more powerful than that of the brain),[7] it pulls or entrains the body's other energy fields into alignment with itself. When we hold a feeling of appreciation in our heart, all other organs, including the brain, begin resonating to the frequency of love. The brain is then less likely to focus on fear and stress and more likely to focus on peace and love.[8]

Moreover, the heart's electromagnetic signal can be felt and measured at a distance of from six to ten feet away. Thus, if your heart rhythm is coherent, this will affect the heart rhythms of other people nearby. So, if you hold your appreciation for a memory of love in your heart for even a few seconds, the increased coherence of your heart rhythm encourages the heart rhythms of those around you to become more coherent as well.[9]

In ordinary life, this simple process has brought healing or improvement in a wide variety of conditions, including congestive heart failure, diabetes, asthma, hypertension, depression, attention deficit disorder (ADD) and hyperactivity (ADHD).[10] Thus, it is not surprising that the immersion in infinite love of the NDE can bring healing to people so sick they have "died."

We Are Love

Not only do NDErs experience healing in the Light of infinite love, but in some of the more extensive NDEs the experiencers realize that they *are* this love. For example, Anita Moorjani had one of the most remarkable documented NDEs on record. She had Stage 4 cancer and was given no hope of recovery. She "died," returned from her NDE, and was almost immediately healed of cancer. In her book, *Dying to Be Me*,[11] she says that she had to die to become herself and realize who she is:

> *Many of us still believe that we have to work at being loving, but that means living in duality because there's a giver and a receiver. Realizing that we are love transcends this. It means understanding that there is no separation between you and me, and if I'm aware that I am love, then I know that you are, too. If I care for myself, then I automatically feel the same for you.*

In my NDE state, I realized that the entire universe is composed of unconditional love, and I'm an expression of this. Every atom, molecule, quark and tetraquark, is made of love. I can be nothing else, because this is my essence and the nature of the entire universe. . . .

. . . when we know that we are love, we don't need to work at being loving toward others. Instead, we just have to be true to ourselves, and we become instruments of loving energy, which touches everyone we come into contact with.[12], **

Thus, Anita's experience is something like a super, meta-memory of peace and love, a greatly intensified experience of holding such a memory in her heart so that it resonated throughout her being, healed her body of a fatal illness, and overcame a lifetime of forgetting her true essence. We imagine that if we were six to ten feet away from Anita, the coherence of her heart would pull our hearts into alignment with the frequency of our essence: love. This, at least, is what we notice in ourselves with friends like Ralph who have had NDEs and report a similar experience of unconditional love so intense that it brought them back from death.

When we get in touch with memories of peace and love, and our hearts resonate to the frequency of love, we are on the path of what Anita experienced in her NDE. We get a glimpse of our true nature and the nature of the universe, which is love. We can grow in this awareness by simply being our real selves. We recall a story told by Ken Ring, in which an NDEr named Virginia visited his university class and shared the ways her experience had changed her life. One of Ken's students,

---

** Elsewhere, Anita clarifies that "One of the insights I gained from being in the full force of love in the other realm is that unconditional love is a state, not an emotion. It's a state of being, and this means it has no opposite. Human love in this physical world is an emotion and, as with all other emotions, it is part of duality. This means it is one side of the coin, and has an opposite emotion to balance it out, such as fear or jealousy. But unconditional love has no opposite—it just is. It's not one side of the coin—it's the whole coin!" Anita Moorjani, "Explaining Unconditional Love," *http://deelmail.blogspot.com/2013/07/explaining-unconditional-love-anita.html* (accessed August 23, 2013).

apparently overcome with "NDE envy," said, "I would love to have an experience like that! But how can I?" Without hesitation, Virginia replied, "Love others."[13] If Virginia had met Anita Moorjani, perhaps Virginia would have said to Ken's student, "Be the love that you are."

This shift in language is somewhat clumsy for us, but we understand why it can be helpful. For example, recently I (Matt) was in the midst of a heated discussion that activated all sorts of negative reactions in me that I struggled to restrain. I began saying silently to myself, "I am love. I am love. I am love," in rhythm with my breathing. Within just a minute I experienced love in my heart, and I responded to the other person in a calm and caring way. Telling myself to give love to the other person would not have helped me find myself in the same way as reminding myself that I am love and all I have to do is be myself.

For me (Sheila), the message of the NDE that I *am* love is profoundly empowering. We used to speak of "giving and receiving love," but I realize that other people don't need for me to *give* them love any more than the ocean needs for me to give it a bucket of water, and vice versa. Therefore, in this book we will use the language of *being* love, in hopes that this will empower our readers and help them remember who they are.

What then do we give and receive with others? We may tend to fall back on the word "love," because this one word means so many things in English. Again, our language is inadequate. Perhaps what we mean can be captured in words like "empathy," "care," "compassion," "kindness," "generosity," "affirmation," "delight in the other," "forgiveness," and the "unconditional positive regard" of which the great psychotherapist Carl Rogers spoke.

For example, a few days ago I (Sheila) was in our local library for a meeting. I felt preoccupied about the meeting, unsure of how to express what I wanted to say. A simply dressed Hispanic woman was standing at the circulation desk, holding the hand of a little girl who appeared to be her grandchild. The woman was trying to check out books for the child. The librarian told the woman that she owed a fine and could not check out anything more until she paid enough of the fine to bring it below $5.00. The woman looked at the librarian and said nothing. To me, her face appeared pale, sad, and hopeless.

As I watched her, I forgot my preoccupation with my meeting. I felt entirely connected and at home within myself. I knew what to do as surely as I know how to breathe: I paid the whole $12.10 fine. The librarian checked out the books and gave them to the woman. At first she seemed a little confused. Then her whole being moved toward me, she put her arms around me and said, "Gracias." I hugged her back and said, "Gracias a ti. Es un honor," meaning, "Thank you. It's an honor." And it was.

I gave compassion and the woman gave gratitude. But really, she gave me an opportunity to be myself, to be the love that I am. And I gave her an opportunity to be the love that she is. The message of the NDE is that we *are* love and whenever we recall a moment of knowing this, we open ourselves to living in the Light.

Remembering Who We Are Through Random Acts of Kindness

When we live in the Light, we are one with everyone else who lives there, in this world and the next. At the memorial service that we (Denny and Sheila) celebrated for Zeke, we wanted a way for the people who came to experience this. The way we found was to invite them to share Zeke's heart and give it away. During his life here, Zeke was a kind boy, full of funny, generous surprises. At his death, his parents donated his heart and other organs, because they knew this is what he would have wanted.

The way in which Zeke gave his heart away reminded us of the Random Acts of Kindness movement, in which a person does something caring and unexpected for another, often a stranger. The classic example is putting change in an expired parking meter for an absent owner who might otherwise get a ticket. So, we asked Zeke's brother, Max, to help design heart-shaped stickers that said, "Love from Zeke." We told our audience that they could stay connected to Zeke through acts of love, for example, by making their sister's bed, washing the dishes when it wasn't their turn, putting a flower or favorite snack in another student's cubby, paying the bill for someone in a restaurant, or any of the other kind, funny, and unexpected things that Zeke would have done. And, we suggested, leave a "Love from Zeke" sticker to show that he was there. We encouraged them to plaster our small town with love from Zeke.

The school had made 2,400 stickers for the memorial service. They ran out of stickers and the next day printed eight thousand more. We wonder if this simple idea caught on because it gave people a concrete way to be the love that they are and to remember that they are one in the Light with Zeke and with each other. Acts of love and memories of love are healing because they help us remember who we are.

Healing Process

We begin each healing process with breathing. Breathing can be a way of getting in touch with our essence and the essence of all things, which is unconditional love. Because air currents cause such a complete mixing of the earth's atmosphere, each time we inhale we take in at least one atom of air breathed by every person on earth within the last few weeks. Since the elements of air circulate through the entire chain of life, breathing is literally a way of connecting ourselves to all of creation. Each time we inhale, we entrain our heart to the universal frequency of unconditional love. Each time we exhale, we connect our unconditional love with that of all creation.

1. Close your eyes and put your feet flat on the floor. Breathe slowly and deeply. Place your hand on your heart and imagine that you are breathing in and out through your heart.

2. Bring to your heart a memory of a moment today or at another time in your life when you lived the love you are. Perhaps it was a moment when you felt especially connected to yourself, another person, or the entire universe. Perhaps you spontaneously reached out to help someone, resonated to the beauty of nature, created something lovely, embraced your spouse or your child, listened deeply to another, shared your heart with someone who took you in . . . whatever moment you get in touch with, imagine you are there again. Hold this memory in your heart and let it grow there.

3. Is there a way you could return to this memory in your everyday life and do more of what enabled you to live the love that you are?

Reflection Questions

What touched me most in this chapter is . . .

When I reflect upon this chapter in relation to my life, I feel . . . I want . . .

≈ 3 ≈

Out of the Body, or
We're Bigger than We Think

In 1989, Olga received a heart transplant. During the operation, all her family members filled the hospital waiting room, except her son-in-law, who had a phobia of hospitals. He waited at home for news of the surgery. At 2:15 a.m., Olga developed complications, the new heart stopped beating, and it took a long period of time for her to be resuscitated. Meanwhile, Olga's family was asleep in the waiting room, entirely unaware of her condition. Around 6:00 a.m., the family heard that the operation was successful, but that Olga had nearly died.

Olga's daughter immediately called her husband to tell him the good news. "I know she's okay," he said. "She already told me herself."

He had awakened at 2:15 [a.m.] to see his mother-in-law standing at the foot of his bed. "It was as though she was standing right there," he said. Thinking she had not had surgery and had somehow come to his house instead, he sat up and asked her how she was.

"I am fine, I'm going to be all right," she said. "There is nothing for any of us to worry about." Then she disappeared.

The vision didn't frighten the son-in-law, but he did get out of bed to write down the time she appeared to him and exactly what was said.

When the family went in to see her, Olga began talking about "the strange dream" that took place during surgery. She said she had left her body and watched the doctors work on her for a few minutes. Then she went into the waiting room, where she saw her family. Frustrated by her inability to communicate with them, she decided to travel to her daughter's home, about thirty miles away, and connect with her son-in-law.

She told them that she was sure she had stood at the foot of her son-in-law's bed and told him that everything was going to be all right.[1]

At least as remarkable as Olga's appearance to her son-in-law is the story of a man who was out driving on an icy road on a dark night and crashed into a tree:

I floated up that tree . . . I was up on top looking down, and I saw my body. An arm was gone and there was blood everywhere. . . . I wanted to save my body . . . so I looked around for help . . . up on a hill I saw a house . . . I floated over to the window and started jumping up and down, screaming as loud as I could: "There's been an accident. Call the police." I repeated this over and over.

The guy inside told the police: "There was this jumping fog outside my window. Fog doesn't jump up and down. I just stared at that fog and then heard a loud voice in my ear, 'There's been an accident. Call the police.' So I called, then

The Gifts of Near-Death Experiences

I grabbed a flashlight and went downstairs. It took me a while to find the wreck."

I was blinded from the impact. The doctors and nurses thought I was hallucinating when I talked about what happened, about being on top of the tree, floating over to the house, jumping up and down, yelling for help. They couldn't shut me up, so they called the guy. He and the police came and confirmed my story—mostly the guy did. Everything is in the accident report. Two months later my sight came back. I used to be a professional artist. My right hand was gone, so I used my left. I said, "get me a pencil and paper." I drew the accident scene, every detail. They called the police and the guy back. They looked at my drawing and said it was totally accurate. People were shocked. It was so dark that night that even a sighted person couldn't have seen the details I did. No one could explain it. [2]

Leaving the Body Is Common in NDEs and Sometimes Verifiable

Near the beginning of a near-death experience, according to Jeffrey Long, 75.4 percent of people leave their bodies as Olga and the Oregon "fog" man did.[3] Cardiologist and near-death researcher Dr. Pim van Lommel describes this as follows:

During an out-of-body experience people have verifiable perceptions from a position outside and above their lifeless body. Patients feel as if they have taken off their body like an old coat, and they are astounded that despite discarding it they have retained their identity, with the faculty of sight, with emotions, and with an extremely lucid consciousness. [4]

Pam Reynolds's experience is one of the most well-documented and impressive cases of being out of the body. She underwent a rare surgical procedure, hypothermic cardiac arrest, to remove a huge and potentially fatal aneurysm from her brain. Her body temperature was lowered to sixty degrees, her breathing and heartbeat were stopped, and her brain was drained of blood. According to the three clinical tests for brain death, her brain was dead. (Her electroencephalogram was silent, her brain-stem response was absent, and there was no blood flow in her brain.) In this state, Pam had an NDE and left her body. She observed and later reported medical procedures she experienced. For example, she gave an accurate description of a unique surgical saw and its case that she had never seen nor heard of before:

> I was metaphorically sitting on [the doctor's] shoulder. It was not like normal vision. It was brighter and more focused and clearer than normal vision. . . . The saw-thing that I hated the sound of looked like an electric toothbrush and it had a dent in it, a groove at the top where the saw appeared to go into the handle, but it didn't. . . . And the saw had interchangeable blades, too, but these blades were in what looked like a socket wrench case.[5]

Perhaps this story impresses us because of the unusual yet easily verifiable nature of the surgical saw that Pam Reynolds described so accurately.

Following are two even more easily verifiable stories, in these cases about shoes. The first was reported by Kimberly Clark, a critical care social worker. Her patient, Maria,

> . . . was a migrant worker who, while visiting friends in Seattle, had a severe heart attack. She was rushed to Harborview Hospital

and placed in the coronary care unit. A few days later she had a cardiac arrest and an unusual out-of-body experience. At one point in this experience, she found herself outside the hospital and spotted a single tennis shoe sitting on the ledge of the north side of the third floor of the building. Maria not only was able to indicate the whereabouts of this oddly situated object, but was able to pro-vide precise details concerning its appearance, such as that its little toe was worn and one of its laces was stuck underneath its heel.

Upon hearing Maria's story, Clark . . . went to the location described to see whether any such shoe could be found. Indeed it was, just where and precisely as Maria had described it, except that from the window through which Clark was able to see it, the details of its appearance that Maria had specified could not be discerned. Clark concluded, "The only way she could have had such a perspective was if she had been floating right outside and at very close range to the tennis shoe."

When Clark retrieved the shoe and brought it back to Maria, the details Maria had provided, such as the blue color, the lace under the heel and the worn place, were confirmed.[6]

As if one misplaced shoe weren't enough, Kenneth Ring reports the following story of another shoe, told to him by Kathy Milne, a nurse at Hartford Hospital. Milne was talking with a patient who had been resuscitated following an NDE:

She told me how she floated up over her body, viewed the resus-citation effort for a short time and then felt herself being pulled up through several floors of the hospital. She then found herself above the roof and realized she was looking at the skyline of Hartford . . . out of the corner of her eye she saw a red object. It turned out to be a shoe. . . . I was relating this to a [skeptical] resident who in a mocking manner left. Apparently, he got a janitor to get him onto the roof. When I saw him later that day, he had a red shoe and became a believer, too.[7]

Just to be sure Kathy Milne had not somehow been influenced by the story of Maria's shoe, Dr. Ring asked Kathy Milne if she had ever heard of it. She had not.[8]

These stories of shoes are significant in that they involve verified experiences of seeing ordinary things that haven't much importance in themselves, but that could only have been seen by the NDErs in an out-of-body state. The story of Dr. George Rodonaia involves seeing something in an out-of-body state that was quite important, in that it led to healing a baby.

George was a Russian physician who had an NDE after the Russian secret police (the KGB) attempted to assassinate him. He was pronounced dead and left in the morgue for three days. He revived as a doctor began to perform an autopsy on him. During his NDE, George visited a nearby hospital where his friend's wife had just given birth to a baby who cried constantly. George knew that in his NDE state he could not communicate with adults, but he could communicate with the baby because, "Children can see and hear spirit beings. The child responded to me because, to her, I was a physical reality."[9] In his NDE state, George was able to scan the baby's body and discover the source of the child's trauma: her hip was broken. He telepathically communicated to the baby that he understood and that she could stop crying. She stopped immediately.

After George returned from his NDE and was revived, he immediately told the child's doctors about her hip. The baby was X-rayed, and George's diagnosis was confirmed. George said, "The hip is broken because the nurse dropped her." A nurse admitted to having dropped the baby and was fired.[10]

Consciousness Transcends Time and Space

All of the above out-of-body experiences (OBEs) occurred during near-death experiences, when the person was immobilized and apparently unconscious. In this condition, how could Pam Reynolds (whose brain was not functioning at all) observe and correctly describe an obscure surgical instrument she had never seen before? How could Maria report the details of a shoe that could only be seen by a person who was hanging in the air outside a third-floor window? How could Kathy Milne's patient, from where her body lay, know there was a red shoe on the roof of the hospital? And how could George diagnose a baby's broken hip in the hospital while his body lay in the morgue? In all of these cases, the consciousness of the person was separated from the brain. There is no medical explanation for this.[11] How is it possible?

Researchers from a wide variety of fields, from quantum physics to near-death studies, share a growing consensus that consciousness, awareness, mind—whatever we wish to call it—transcends the physical brain and can function independently of it. Dr. Pim van Lommel is one of many scientists who believe that the brain neither produces consciousness nor stores memories. He cites Simon Berkovich (an American computer science expert) and Herms Romijn (a Dutch brain researcher), who independently concluded that

> . . . it is impossible for the brain to store everything you think and experience in your life. This would require a processing speed of 1024 bits per second. Simply watching an hour of television would already be too much for our brains. "If you want to store that amount of information—along with the associative thoughts produced—your brain would be pretty much full," van Lommel says. "Anatomically and functionally, it is simply impossible for the brain to have this level of speed." So this would mean that the

brain is actually a receiver and transmitter of information. "You could compare the brain to a television set that tunes into specific electromagnetic waves and converts them into image and sound, [says van Lommel].[12, *]

Researchers who agree that conscious awareness transcends the physical brain have described consciousness as the ground of all being, prior to matter, unitive, and non-local.[**] These traits of consciousness can help us understand a different way of perceiving and knowing during OBEs that is independent of the brain and of the sense organs as well. Kenneth Ring calls it "transcendental awareness," which is "more a realm of knowledge than a type of perception as such." In the case of seeing, this "involves seeing in detail, sometimes from all angles at once, with everything in focus, and a sense of 'knowing' the subject, not just visually, but with multi-sensory knowledge."[13]

---

[*] "But how does the brain "know" what information to tune into? How can someone tune into his own memories and not those of other people? Van Lommel's answer is . . . DNA. And primarily the so-called 'junk DNA,' which accounts for around 95 percent of the total whose function we don't understand." He suspects that the DNA, unique to every person and every organism, works like a receptor mechanism, a kind of simultaneous translator between the information fields of the organism.

"The idea that DNA works as a receptor mechanism to attune people to their specific consciousness fields sheds new light on the discussion of organ transplantation. Imagine you get a new heart. The DNA of that heart will gear itself to the consciousness field of the donor, not the recipient. Does this mean you suddenly get new information? "Yes," van Lommel says: "There are stories of people who developed radically different desires and lifestyles after an organ transplant. For example, there's a story of a ballet dancer who suddenly wanted to drive a motorcycle and eat junk food." Tijn Touber, "A New Lease on Life," interview with Pim van Lommel, *http://www.theosociety.org/pasadena/sunrise/55-05-6/de-touber.htm* (accessed May 10, 2013); originally published in *Ode*, 3(10), December, 2005.

[**] Traits of consciousness include (1) Consciousness is the ground of all being, meaning that "all reality is comprised of consciousness." (2) Consciousness is primary, meaning that it is prior to matter (rather than arising from matter). Thus, consciousness gives rise to the matter of the brain rather than vice versa. (3) Consciousness is unitive, meaning that "there is only one consciousness, which we call Mind, and the notion of individual minds is at bottom nothing more than a useful fiction . . ." (4) Because it is prior to and greater than all the categories we normally use to construct reality, such as space and time, consciousness is non-local. It transcends space and time. See Kenneth Ring & Sharon Cooper, *Mindsight: Near-Death and Out-of-Body Experiences in the Blind*, Second Edition (New York: iUniverse, Inc., 2008), 113.

Blind people who don't even see in their dreams, including those blind from birth, can do this. Not only do they observe the visual details of their own medical treatment, which they can later describe correctly, but they also perceive the beings of Light, deceased loved ones and other visual aspects of the NDE. For example, Vicki, who had two NDEs, reported, "Those two experiences were the only time I could ever relate to seeing, and to what light was, because I experienced it. I was able to see."[14]

As Pam Reynolds (who is not blind) describes it, "It was not like normal vision. It was brighter and more focused and clearer than normal vision . . ." In other words, although the ability of people blind from birth to "see" during an OBE seems especially impressive, it really only highlights a capacity we all have that far transcends anything we normally think of as sight.

Thus, Maria found herself eyeing a tennis shoe on a third-floor window ledge as if she were suspended in the air. In the following account, the great psychiatrist Carl Jung looked down on the earth from one thousand miles above it, a vantage point that no human had yet visited. In 1944, Jung had a heart attack and an NDE. He left his body and saw the earth from outer space. Although it would be two decades before astronauts saw it from this vantage point, Jung was able to describe the earth with remarkable accuracy:

> It seemed to me that I was high up in space. Far below I saw the globe of the Earth, bathed in a gloriously blue light. I saw the deep blue sea and the continents. Far below my feet lay Ceylon, and in the distance ahead of me the subcontinent of India. My field of vision did not include the whole Earth, but its global shape was plainly distinguishable and its outlines shone with a silvery gleam through that wonderful blue light. In many places the globe seemed colored, or spotted dark green like oxidized silver. Far away to the left lay a broad expanse—the reddish-yellow desert of Arabia; it was as though the silver of the Earth had there assumed a reddish-gold hue. Then came the Red Sea, and far, far back—as

if in the upper left of a map—I could just make out a bit of the Mediterranean. . . . I could also see the snow-covered Himalayas, but in that direction it was foggy or cloudy. . . .

Later I discovered how high in space one would have to be to have so extensive a view—approximately a thousand miles! The sight of the Earth from this height was the most glorious thing I have ever seen.[15]

Jung saw the earth from a thousand miles away. Impressive as this is, sometimes out-of-body experiences and the transcendental awareness they involve can lead to "cosmic consciousness," in which one goes even further than Jung and merges with all of reality. For example, during his NDE, Mellen-Thomas Benedict's consciousness left the earth and traveled beyond everything we know of time and space:

It seemed as if all the creations in the universe soared by me and vanished in a speck of light. . . . I could see or perceive FOREVER, beyond infinity. . . . I was in pre-creation, before the Big Bang. I had crossed over the beginning of time. . . . Simply I was at one with absolute life and consciousness.[16]

As Mellen-Thomas Benedict experienced, the consciousness of each one of us is as big . . . bigger . . . than the entire universe. We are all out of our bodies, so to speak, in that we are infinitely bigger than our physical container.

Unlimited Possibilities

This sense of unlimited possibility that many NDErs find in an out-of-body experience can be profoundly healing and empowering for anyone. Most evenings, we (Denny and Sheila) feel something similar as we swing in our hammock and explore the starlit night sky.

The stars remind us that we were born at the Big Bang, or what many call the "Great Radiance" because it was a great pouring forth of the photons that comprise light. The hydrogen that formed then clumped together and eventually ignited into stars. The other elements that comprise our bodies came from the explosion of these stars. We are, literally, made of stardust. We were there when plants figured out photosynthesis, when fish formed, and when humans first stood erect. In our consciousness is the history of the entire universe, and we carry within us the wisdom of 13.8 billion years. Every star reminds us of our original home—that we, too, were once a star. And so every night we ponder: How did we get from the heart of those great glowing stars to swinging in this hammock now in our very own backyard? If we could do that, anything must be possible!

One night, as we left the starlit sky and came inside, we tried to hold on to our sense of awe and unlimited possibilities as we helped John prepare invitations to his birthday party. We wondered, "What will John's future be like?" Supposing we had television and had sat down to watch the newscasters with their nightly lists of wars and other tragedies or the advertisements trying to sell us remedies for the next deadly disease waiting to get us? In a short while, we might have lost our sense of possibilities given by the starlit sky.

Instead, as we addressed envelopes for John's invitations, we recalled what gives us hope whenever we worry about his future: two photos of John just after he was born. The first photo, taken in the hospital, shows a tiny but determined baby, with light beaming from his eyes and a fist raised, as if nothing is going to stop him. John loves this photo and has it in a frame beside his bed. We bring this first photo of John to our seminars and compare it to a second photo, also taken shortly after John's birth.

This second photo is projected on a screen during our entire program. Entitled "Seven Year Microwave Sky," and taken by the Wilkenson Microwave Anisotropy Probe, this photo shows the oldest light in the universe, or how John and all the rest of us looked at the young age of 380,000 years old.[17] That light has been John for more than thirteen billion years. Its determination helped him survive the explosion of the stars and then guided him safely to us. That same light beamed from his eyes seventeen years ago as he raised a determined fist. Now, it gives us hope that our 13.8-billion-year-old son embodies all the light and wisdom that he needs. That's a birth worth celebrating.

One NDEr describes it this way:

> I understood the origins of the cosmos. . . . I saw evolution. Everything and everyone evolves and develops together. . . . I knew and understood all about mathematics, electronics, physics, DNA, atoms, quantum mechanics and quantum physics. . . . I also saw where evolution is headed, what its ultimate goal is. I realized that this grand scheme not only includes me, but everything and everybody, every human being, every soul, every animal, every cell, the earth and every other planet, the universe, the cosmos, the Light. Everything is connected and everything is one.[18]

In the sense that consciousness researchers usually mean it, 10 percent of Americans have had out-of-body experiences, and most of them occurred outside of near-death experiences.[19] But, in the sense of our 13.8-billion-year history, we've all been out of our bodies a lot more than we've been in them.

Healing Process

1. Close your eyes and put your feet flat on the floor. Breathe slowly and deeply. Place your hand on your heart and imagine that you are breathing in and out through your heart.

2. Leonardo Boff reminds us that,

> *All of us are beings of light. We were originally formed in the heart of the great red stars, thousands of millions of years ago. We carry light within us, in our bodies, in our hearts and in our minds.*[20]

Get in touch with the Light within yourself that you are emitting from each of your trillions of cells. See the Light coalesce into the radiance that you are.

3. As you breathe out, see the Light extend beyond your body, growing bigger and bigger until it surrounds the entire earth. With each breath out, continue to extend it beyond our solar system, beyond our galaxy and out to the furthest reaches of the universe. Send this Light backward to the beginning of time and forward into eternity.

4. Rest for a while, experiencing your true size.

Reflection Questions

What touched me most in this chapter is . . .

When I reflect upon this chapter in relation to my life, I feel . . . I want . . .

∼ 4 ∼

Through the Tunnel:
Healing Transitions

. . . my consciousness traveled while my body remained motion-less on the bed. I could see my body but I couldn't feel it. I was being sucked away, as it were. I entered an extremely dark, long and spiral-shaped tunnel. . . . I soared through this spiral-shaped funnel, and the further or the higher I got, the lighter it became. The intensity of the light changed to a deep purple/violet. "Above" me I saw an extremely bright, radiant white light. I whirled, floated toward it.[1]

Then I remember a very powerful force pulling me towards a serene, very beautiful realm, a higher realm. I traveled very slowly along a tunnel toward a bright light, and I could feel an overwhelming sense of warmth and peace and whiteness. I wanted to walk into the whiteness, which was so tranquil and happy. . . . I felt okay, as though this was where I was meant to be, as if I had arrived home, and I was at ease with myself for the first time in a long time.[2]

At this point I became aware that there was a light calling me from somewhere else and I entered what people speak of as the tunnel. . . . It was a transition place. . . .[3]

One of the most widely known images of a near-death experience is passing through a tunnel after leaving one's body. According to Jeffrey Long, "entering a tunnel/dark void" occurs in about 34 percent of NDEs.[4, *]

Sometimes a tunnel experience is shared, as in the following example of a husband whose wife was dying:

As he held her in her final moments, a bright light filled the room. . . . He saw it as "the brightest light I'd ever seen," yet at the same time, something that seemed more like "plasma or the kind of light you see when you get snow-blinded."

This light was present for everyone in the room . . . but this man had a particularly vivid experience. As he was holding his wife when she passed away, he felt himself racing up a tunnel as she died. Then . . . he could feel her pass through him and into a bright light that glowed at the end of the tunnel.[5]

---

* A small percentage of NDEs involve a frightening experience, sometimes in the tunnel. Pim van Lommel estimates that frightening NDEs occur about 1 to 2 percent of the time. Kenneth Ring estimates it at 5 percent. Dr. Ring believes that negative experiences are usually truncated NDEs and often resolve themselves into the typical and much more common radiant and ecstatic NDE when the person meets the Light or has some other positive experience. Jeffrey Long agrees that most "frightening" NDEs develop into the typical "blissful, positive" experience that is "full of light and love." Long estimates truly "hellish" NDEs at less than 1 percent. He reports that people who have such an experience often reflect upon it later as the only way they could have learned something they needed to know in order to make a change for the good in their life. Mainstream researchers give varying explanations for frightening or hellish NDEs, but they emphasize that such experiences should not be taken as proof of "hell." To the contrary, the consensus of mainstream researchers is that NDEs indicate that no one is ever lost. Kenneth Ring, personal correspondence, September 1, 2013; see also Pim van Lommel, *Consciousness Beyond Life* (New York: HarperCollins, 2010), 11, 29–31, and Interview with Jeffrey Long, "Is There Life After Death? Scientific Research Facts," *https://www .youtube.com/watch?v=7HhOZLN_9FM* (accessed May 31, 2015).

Tunnels

As they cross over from this world to the next, it doesn't surprise us that many NDErs describe the tunnel as "a transition place." Tunnels and transitions seem to go hand in hand. For example, we (Denny and Sheila) just returned from a graduation at our son's school, where the final part of the ceremony was a tunnel formed by the teachers, families, and other friends through which the graduates passed. As they emerged from the end of the tunnel, more welcoming friends embraced them.

When I (Denny) think of the biggest transition in my life, it was when I got married. By then, I had spent many years in a celibate Jesuit community. During almost that entire time, I never imagined that I would get married (or experience the other transitions that, for me, went with marriage, such as paying taxes, purchasing a home and a car, or having a child). When we were helping to form the tunnel for graduates at our son's school, I was reminded of the tunnel that friends formed for Sheila and me at the end of our wedding ceremony.

Transitions

Tunnels represent a transition from one state of being into another that often includes a period of not knowing where one is or where one is going. It is a journey from familiar reality, through darkness, and into light. We have all made such a journey many times in our lives. The darkness may be anything from mild discomfort to acute suffering, or it may be simply the uncertainty and even blind excitement of not knowing exactly where we are headed.

We suspect that many, perhaps most, of our readers are at the beginning, middle, or end of a life transition. Perhaps you are entering a marriage or other significant relationship; perhaps you are leaving one. Perhaps you are beginning a new career or about to retire. Perhaps you have a new baby or your child is about to leave home. Perhaps you are moving from adolescence to young adulthood, from young adulthood to mid-life, and so on. Whatever the transition, the underlying dynamic of letting go of a familiar way of being, experiencing the unknown, and opening ourselves to a new way of being is similar.

What Helps Us Move Through Transitions?

In a near-death experience, we get a glimpse of what it is like to make the greatest and most universal human transition after birth, which is death. A very high percentage of NDErs report losing their fear of death. We are not aware of research demonstrating that their fear of other transitions is diminished as well, but we might hypothesize that this is the case.

Thus, the NDE may hold clues as to what can help us through all the transitions in life. What is it about the NDE that heals fear of the transition of death? A clue comes from our observation that, in general, NDErs' tunnel accounts are relatively short. For example, we just watched over one hundred videos of NDErs sharing their experiences, as we searched for videos that we could use in the seminar that accompanies this book. We had trouble finding extensive tunnel accounts, because as soon as NDErs began talking about the tunnel (or however they described it—for example, as a dark passage way), they almost immediately started talking about the light they spotted at the end of it. This welcoming light, sometimes radiating from flowers, trees, animals, and the natural surroundings, at other times radiating from friends and relatives or a being of Light, seemed to heal their fear of death as they transitioned from this world to the next.

It seems that the Light, regardless of what it radiates from, is the key to experiencing a healing transition. Perhaps that is because the Light reminds us of who we are. Many NDErs experience that the Light at the end of the tunnel, the infinite and unconditionally loving Light that awaits us, is us . . . our real self. A transition requires that we let go of something, but, ultimately, it is our real self that we do not want to lose. The NDEr realizes that his or her real self is not any of the attachments we form in this life to give ourselves identity: attachments to our bodies and physical abilities; to our relationships with others; to our roles, careers, possessions, and social status; and so forth. Our real self is the loving Light. It seems that what facilitates a healthy transition is anything that helps us access and stay connected to that loving Light that we are.

Like NDErs transitioning through the tunnel, the Light radiating from natural surroundings and from the unconditional love of welcoming friends helped me (Denny) make a healthy transition toward marriage. At that time, a snow-covered farm field helped me stay in touch with my Light. (See Chapter 5.) Also, although I had many unconditionally loving friends, a community in St. Louis was particularly important. Even though it meant a two-thousand-mile trip, every year for the next sixteen years we would celebrate our wedding anniversary with them. Welcoming friends and memories of the snow-covered farm field still continue to help me stay connected during transitions to the loving Light that I am.

Birth: A Template for the Transition of Death

The first time we pass through a tunnel is at birth. Even if we were born by caesarean section and did not literally traverse a tunnel, we passed from one mode of existence into another. Thus, we might consider birth, our primal transition, as a metaphor or template for all other transitions in life, including the transition of death.

The metaphor of birth seems helpful for healing transitions, not only in that it parallels the experience of passing through a tunnel from the familiar to the unknown, but also in that it normally is preceded by the experience of being held in all-embracing love in the womb. Consider the following excerpt from an NDE, in which the experiencer rests in a womb-like place before he is ready to move through the tunnel and into the Light:

I was no longer able to see my body in the X-ray room. I was still out of my body, but now I had no sight. My world was utter darkness. I sensed myself but nothing was there. . . . There was an indescribable feeling of love and warmth. It could be like a child before birth in its mother's womb. I felt nothing but peace and tranquility. I never wanted to leave—it was as if I was searching for this place my whole life.[6]

In her work with a cancer patient who was not in the midst of an NDE but who was in a transition in the sense of coming to terms with his illness, Dr. Rachel Naomi Remen accompanied him as he found this same place of peace and safety:

. . . caught up in rage at cancer and its treatment, [he] responded to the question "What do you think may be needed for your healing?" with a terse "Nothing!" Taking his statement at face value, I asked him to describe "nothing" to me. "Unending darkness," he said. . . . I encouraged him to close his eyes and experience it.

As his face became more and more relaxed, I asked him how he was feeling. . . .

"The darkness is all around me. . . .

I'm not falling. It holds me. I am held in darkness.

Wrapped in darkness.

The darkness is . . . soft . . . almost tender.

It's safe here.

I needed to feel safe. I haven't relaxed since I got the diagnosis. I can rest. I am so tired.

No pain here. No hunger. No need."

After a while, he commented that he could hear a sound "like a great heartbeat." It was deeply comforting.

*I encouraged him to lean up against it. To rest. Soon he began to
weep softly, saying, "Mama, mama. . . ."*

*. . . Darkness is a condition of the beginning. The body first
comes into being in darkness. It is nurtured, as a seed, in darkness. Some people may find their healing in remembering the
beginning.*[7]

Healing Process: A Loving Tunnel

Following is a process that uses the safety of the womb and
experience of birth as a metaphor or image for any transition in
life. To the extent that we feel safe and cared for, we can move
through the developmental stages and experiences of life with
trust and courage.

1. Close your eyes and put your feet flat on the floor. Breathe
    slowly and deeply. Place your hand on your heart and
    imagine that you are breathing in and out through your
    heart. With each breath, let your awareness grow that you
    are love.

2. Let yourself grow younger and younger, smaller and smaller,
    until you are the size you were on the day you were born.
    Imagine yourself inside your mother's womb (or inside the
    womb of the most loving mother you can imagine), ready to
    begin the journey through the birth canal.

3. Imagine the world outside and how you would like it to be.

    Where would be a safe place for your mother? Imagine her
    there.

    If you wish, ask yourself where would you like your father to
    be in relation to your mother? Imagine him there.

    Who (from any time in your life) would you like to be present
    to support your birth and welcome you? Imagine these
    people touching your mother gently, gazing at her lovingly,

encouraging and cheering for her—giving her whatever she needs to feel calm, confident, and ready to receive you into her arms.

4. As your mother takes in what she needs, feel the good energy of the hormones associated with these positive emotions coming into you through the umbilical cord—it is the most nourishing, best-tasting, healthiest food you could imagine.

5. When you are ready to begin your journey, notice that the birth canal is exactly as you need it to be so that you can pass through it. It is flexible enough so that you can move, yet firm enough to support you. It is wide enough for you, yet offers just enough resistance so that you can feel your power as you push your way through. Meanwhile, feel your mother's body moving in rhythm with yours so that the two of you are dancing together. See her pelvic bones opening wide as you pass through them into the light beyond.

6. See the people around your mother and let the radiant face of each one tell you how very glad he or she is that you are born.

7. Rest in your mother's arms and the loving presence of your father.

8. If you wish, as the adult you are, let your mother give you that child to welcome and care for.

Now imagine a similar process at the end of your life, when you will go on another journey into a new world:

1. Close your eyes and put your feet flat on the floor. Breathe slowly and deeply. Place your hand on your heart and imagine that you are breathing in and out through your heart. With each breath, let your awareness grow that you are love.

2. Let yourself grow older and older, moving through this life, until you are ready to pass on to the next one.

3. Imagine the ideal setting for this passage.

   Who (from any time in your life) would you like present to support your passage? Imagine these people gathered around you, touching you gently, gazing at you lovingly, encouraging and cheering for you. They are giving you whatever you need to feel calm, confident, and ready.

4. When you are ready to begin your journey, see yourself entering a tunnel that is exactly as you need it to be. Let yourself relax, let go and pass through it safely, trusting that the loving environment you have left is only a shadow of the one that awaits you.

Reflection Questions

What touched me most in this chapter is . . .

When I reflect upon this chapter in relation to my life, I feel . . . I want . . .

☙ 5 ☙

Sacred Space

Everything in the home from which we came and the home to which we are going is alive and made of love. In the example below, during her NDE, Laura perceived herself as one with and loved by even the flowers:

> My surroundings were then brought into focus as I became aware of a flower. A magnificent flower . . . rather like a perfect Gerber Daisy glowing in brilliant orange-hued colors. And it was alive, and it was loving me! In amazement I turned again to him [her guide] in wonderment and awe, exclaiming, "This flower is loving me, I can feel it." "Everything," he said, "was made in love for you." Then I saw and felt all. It was me and I was it. The firmament with colors alive—loving, stunning colors of light. Water—each drop alive and loving.[1]

Vicki, who was blind and never saw light, even in her dreams, was able to see during her NDE and described what she saw as follows:

*Everybody there was made of light. And I was made of light.
What the light conveyed was love. There was love everywhere. It
was like love came from the grass, love came from the birds, love
came from the trees.*[2]

Following is another account of intense natural beauty, in
this case during a shared-death experience:

*[A] friend with leukemia came to me in a sort of vision. I could
see me with him. He said, "Come, my friend, walk with me."
And we walked through a beautiful forest and came upon a ridge
that looked into the most beautiful valley I have ever thought
about seeing. It sort of glowed and sparkled. He said, "This is as
far as you can go," and he walked off into this valley and I felt
immensely peaceful. It still brings tears to my eyes; I will never
forget it. The next day his daughter-in-law called and told me he
had died the night before.*[3]

We felt surprised and comforted when we first read such
accounts of living things, such as flowers, trees, meadows, mountains, dogs, and butterflies occurring in NDEs. The surprise was
because we had thought of the next life as somehow purely "spiritual" and not composed of everyday material things, like plants
or "lower creatures," such as dogs. (See Chapter 7.) We felt
comforted to think we might be wrong, because we love nature
so much and feel happy to think that we'll enjoy it forever.

The following account, by NDEr Eben Alexander, is one of
the most beautiful descriptions we have read of how nature on
this side is a glimpse of what is to come:

*The worlds above are not general, not vague. They are deeply,
piercingly alive. . . .*

*There are trees in the worlds above this one. There are fields,
and there are animals and people. There is water, too—water*

in abundance. It flows in rivers and descends as rain. Mists rise from the pulsing surfaces of these waters, and fish glide beneath them. Not abstract, mathematical fish, either. Real ones. Every bit as real as any fish you've seen, and way, way more so. The waters there are like earthly water. And yet they're not earthly water. They are . . . more than simply earthly water. It's water that is closer to the source. Closer, like the water higher up on a meandering river is closer to the springs from which it emerges. It's water that's deeply familiar—so that when you see it you realize that all the most beautiful waterscapes you ever saw on earth were beautiful precisely because they were reminding you of it. It's living water, the way everything is living up there. . . .

When we ascend, in short, everything's still there. Only it's more real. Less dense, yet at the same time more intense—more there.[4]

What Kind of Park System Is There on the Other Side?

The story of four-year-old Tom illustrates just how similar nature in the other realm is to the natural things around us. A few months after Tom had experienced an NDE while undergoing intestinal surgery, his father asked Tom where he might like to go that day. Tom responded that he wanted to go back to "that park." When asked which park, Tom responded, "The one through the tunnel that I went to when I was in the hospital. There was a park with lots of children and swings and things, with a white fence around it." Tom explained how he had tried to climb over the fence and, after someone told him not to do it, he found himself back in the hospital again. Tom had no problem thinking that the park was just like any normal park that he and his father might visit that day.[5]

Jan, an adult who had an NDE, describes a similar children's park. "Children were playing on a grassy expanse leading to a small pond. Ducks were swimming in the water. Some sort of game was being played . . . a follow-the-leader type of thing."[6]

We wonder if it was the same park that Tom described, or if on the other side there is an immense park system that matches our own?

When we realize that the flowers, trees, parks, and other natural things around us in this life are at least similar to the "stuff" of the other realm, such things become a window into another way of being. For example, for many years I (Denny) have jogged along a path that cuts through a pine forest. Since catching the benign virus, I find the jog to be quite different. Today, for example, I noticed a lone pine still standing in the midst of three fallen ones. I asked how it felt, and it seemed to me that I felt the pine's sadness at being the only one left alive, as well as its love and appreciation that I had cared enough to ask. When I jog now, I still enjoy the beauty, but now I take in how each thing (a tree, a rock, a stream) is alive and loving me. As I jog, I wonder to myself, "Do I feel so at home in myself when I jog because it reminds me of where I came from and where I am going?" Could this recognition of home be why I am so drawn to forests, parks, streams, and other places of beauty?

What Are Natural Images in NDEs Trying to Tell Us?

Is the perception of nature in an NDE how things in this world really are, if only we could see them in their essence in ordinary life? Consider the following account by Eruera, who was severely injured during a rugby game:

> Instantly I was thrust outside of my body and was immediately looking at my body . . . . I could tell that it was in a state of trauma. . . . I became further aware of what was happening around my body and [of] my awareness capacity. For instance, when I looked at the grass I could tell that it was grass but there was an element present that had been missing for the short duration of my physical existence, that element was love. The grass was me and I was the grass, the grass was aware of me, and I

had just become aware of the grass. Another example was when I . . . made a conscious decision to look at the trees because there was an aura of warmth and care emanating from that direction. When I looked at the trees again they were aware of me; exuding from the trees was love and acceptance.[7]

I (Sheila) understand this because I have had very similar experiences. When I was a child, I used to go walking in the woods that adjoined our neighborhood. Often I would notice a leaf or a blade of grass, and I would sit there for what seemed like hours, looking at that leaf or blade of grass, noticing its utter goodness. As I attended to it, I would see how radiant it was and how full of personal, loving presence. The leaf or blade of grass had become a revelation of something infinite. Sometimes at a certain point there would be a shift, and I would sense that presence looking back at me, as if trying to assure me of my own goodness.

What Sheila saw in a leaf or blade of grass and the accounts of natural images in NDEs raise many questions for us. For example, are elements of nature included in an NDE to help us feel more at home in the other realm, as a thoughtful host or hostess might decorate a guest bedroom with objects familiar to the guest? However we explain it, natural objects are a common element in NDEs and experiencing this directly in one's own NDE or learning about others' experiences of this seem to deepen our awareness that we are one with all of life. For example, Mary Grace describes the sense of union with all creation that she experienced following her NDE. It included

. . . the trees, the plants, the animals, the birds and even the insects. I soon discovered that I could merge with all this life and love that surrounded me. This meant that many of the physical laws no longer applied to me. For example, I discovered that I could leave my body at will to feel what it was like to soar with.

*the bald eagles over Hemlock Lake, or to bob up and down with
the Canadian geese surfing the waves. I could become one with a
ripple of water and feel what it was like to drift down a stream.*[8]

Similarly, following is an account of returning from an NDE
by a man whom Raymond Moody describes as "a hard-driving,
no nonsense businessman":

*The first thing I saw when I awoke [from my NDE] in the hos-
pital was a flower, and I cried. Believe it or not, I had never
really seen a flower until I came back from death. One big thing
I learned when I died was that we are all part of one big, living
universe. If we think we can hurt another person or another living thing without hurting ourselves, we are sadly mistaken. I look
at a forest or a flower or a bird now, and say, "That is me, part
of me."*[9]

After learning about such experiences, I (Matt) was out in
Denny and Sheila's front yard. I had gone there to dig up weeds,
especially dandelions. However, I kept thinking of the story at
the beginning of this chapter about the woman who felt loved
by flowers during her NDE. I realized I could no longer think of
dandelions as "weeds." Instead, I felt one with them and quite
respectful of how tenacious they are. They now seemed more
like "super plants" than pests.

I recalled our friend, Ken McAll, who had been a prisoner
of war in Japan during World War II. He and his family survived
on the dandelions growing in the prison compound. After Ken
was released and moved back to a large home on many acres of
land in England, he forbade anyone to dig up a dandelion on
his property. Instead, he harvested the leaves and served them
in salad every night for dinner. Perhaps the dandelions greeted
Ken when he died and communicated their love and gratitude.

The Gifts of Near-Death Experiences

Creating a Sacred Space

People who have had NDEs tend to be especially sensitive to their physical environment after they return. They are less able to tolerate anything that is inconsistent with the intensely vital, life-giving energy of the other realm. Thus, they have more adverse reactions to pharmaceuticals, other drugs, and alcohol than previously. Many avoid foods that contain chemicals or artificial sweeteners and prefer organic foods instead. Some become vegetarians. They seek out nature and fresh air.[10]

This sensitivity extends to sounds. Many NDEs include music, and NDErs typically feel drawn to music that resonates with their experience. They prefer natural, gentle, melodious sounds and take more pleasure than before in classical or soothing music. They dislike loud, jarring noise.[11] NDE researcher P. M. H. Atwater writes,

> Of the three thousand plus experiencers I have spoken with, I have only met one who could tolerate rock music after undergoing the near-death phenomenon. . . . The rest can't stand the stuff anymore, even if they were aficionados previously. I can't begin to emphasize how tonal people become afterward, and how emotionally affected they are by sounds. To say that music preferences change is an understatement.[12],*

Whether or not we have had an NDE, most of us are affected by our physical surroundings. Because of this, during our seminars we are careful to create a beautiful and nourishing space for our participants. We arrange the chairs in semi-circles rather

---

* In the popular imagination of those who believe in an afterlife, it often includes exquisitely beautiful "celestial" music. Many NDEs do include this. For example, Eben Alexander reports, "I remember gold and silver arcs, sparkling trails. And from these arcs were coming these anthems, these choral hymns . . . the power behind that music, so infinite and awe-inspiring music, more beautiful than anything I could imagine on earth." Wisconsin Public Radio, *To the Best of Our Knowledge*, "Transcript for Eben Alexander on Near Death Experience," *http://ttbook.org/book/transcript/transcript-eben-alexander-near-death-experience* (accessed May 15, 2013).

than straight lines because the roundedness seems to soften the whole environment. We ask for flowers or plants around the area where we will be speaking. We request healthy snacks and ask our hosts to avoid all toxic foods, such as artificial sweeteners, GMOs (genetically modified organisms), and chemical preservatives.** We choose melodious, nurturing music and find that a single well-played piano, flute, or guitar is far more healing than a big music group with electronic instruments. We are trying to create a beautiful, if temporary, home where our guests can experience their goodness and beauty because the surroundings mirror who they are.

Many of us do the same in our own homes. When we thoughtfully arrange our space, choose decorations with care, plant gardens, hang wind chimes, prepare nutritious meals or otherwise make our surroundings beautiful and physically nurturing, perhaps we are intuitively recalling where we came from and where we are going. Whether or not we have had an NDE, we can replicate the next world because it is us. And, we suspect that the more carefully and consciously we create an environment of beauty around ourselves, the more likely we are to catch the benign virus.

Sacred Spaces Heal Us

As I mentioned in Chapter 4, I (Denny) lived for many years in a celibate Jesuit community, and I had many fears in making

---

** Our concern about this seems consistent with the accounts of some NDErs. For example, Amy reports that she saw the earth and "There were fields of crops all over. . . . As I would zoom in and get close, for instance, to a field of wheat, I would be told, 'This has been poisoned. The food has been altered and poisoned. It is no longer pure. The people are consuming impure food. This is death.' I felt sad and concerned about this and wondered why . . . or how it was possible. How could a field of wheat or corn by 'poisoned' . . . and WHY? I was told that man should return to the Earth or death would ensue everywhere. . . . I was told that upon my return, I should look for pure food, unadulterated . . . and only consume that which is 'clean,' but I dismissed this somewhat, because I had no intention of returning." *http://www.nderf.org/NDERF/ amy_c_nde_4720.htm* (accessed July 31, 2012).

what would be the biggest transition in my life: the transition to marriage.

One day as I sat before a large window watching the snow fall gently on farm fields, the peace of the snowy scene came inside me. The peaceful fields seemed to be saying to me, "We are your brothers and sisters. Just as we have been cared for all those years, so will you." I felt a change throughout my body; my back seemed to straighten and I felt taller. It was as if every cell believed the message of the peaceful fields. I now had the freedom to make the transition toward marriage. I could have spent years trying to heal all the hurts behind my fears, but I doubt I would have received what was given to me by nature in those moments.

Healing Process

1. Close your eyes and put your feet flat on the floor. Breathe slowly and deeply. Place your hand on your heart and imagine that you are breathing in and out through your heart. With each breath, let your awareness grow that you are love.

2. In your imagination, create a sacred space for yourself. Include whatever speaks to you of beauty, love, goodness, and vibrant life.

3. Imagine yourself in this setting. Be aware that everything around you is alive and loving you.

4. Rest in the awareness that you are what you see in this sacred space.

5. You may wish to rest in this sacred space before you fall asleep at night and recall it again when you wake up in the morning.

Reflection Questions

What touched me most in this chapter is . . .

When I reflect upon this chapter in relation to my life, I feel . . . I want . . .

$\backsim$ 6 $\backsim$

Meeting Loved Ones: People

The greatest hurt for most people is the loss of a loved one. Following a death, the universal question in the human heart is, "Will I ever see this person again?" When we love someone deeply, it seems impossible and incomprehensible that he or she, and the world between us created by our relationship, is gone forever. We may tell ourselves to get over it, but something within us insists that real love can never end. Perhaps that is why stories of reunions with loved ones who have passed on to the next life are so moving and comforting for us.

Studies find that up to about half of people who have NDEs report encountering other beings, most often loved ones, on the other side.[1] For example, Dr. Elisabeth Kubler-Ross recounts the story of a man who had lost his wife and children in a car accident. He had no other close relatives and felt entirely overwhelmed by shock and grief. He became a drug-addicted, alcoholic, suicidal bum, trying to die so he could be reunited with his family. After two years of this, as he lay on the side of a road, a truck ran over him. He watched the accident from a few feet above his body:

It was at this moment that his family appeared in front of him, in a glow of light with an incredible sense of love. They had happy smiles on their faces, and simply made him aware of their presence, not communicating in any verbal way but in the form of thought transference, sharing with him the joy and happiness of their present existence. . . . He was so awed by his family's health, their beauty, their radiance and their total acceptance of this present situation, by their unconditional love. He made a vow not to touch them, not to join them, but to re-enter his physical body so that he could share with the world what he had experienced. It would be a form of redemption for his two years of trying to throw his physical life away. It was after this vow that he watched the truck driver carry his totally injured body into the car. He saw an ambulance speeding to the scene of the accident, he was taken to the hospital's emergency room and he finally re-entered his physical body, tore off the straps that were tied around him and literally walked out of the emergency room. He never had delirium tremens or any aftereffects from the heavy abuse of drugs and alcohol. He felt healed and whole, and made a commitment that he would not die until he had the opportunity of sharing the existence of life after death with as many people as would be willing to listen. It was after reading a newspaper article about my appearance in Santa Barbara that he sent a message to the auditorium. By [my] allowing him to share with my audience, he was able to keep the promise he made at the time of his short, temporary, yet happy reunion with his entire family.[2]

The relatives on the other side who appear during an NDE may be not only immediate family members, as in the story above, but also more distant relatives and ancestors:

Then I looked to my left and saw my grandmother who had passed away when I was nine months old. I also saw all of my deceased relatives with her, thousands of them. They were in translucent spirit form.[3]

The family members encountered by an NDEr may have been unknown during this life but are later identified, for example, in family photos.

During my NDE following a cardiac arrest, I saw both my dead grandmother and a man who looked at me lovingly but whom I didn't know. Over ten years later my mother confided on her deathbed that I'd been born from an extramarital affair; my biological father was a Jewish man who'd been deported and killed in World War II. My mother showed me a photograph. The unfamiliar man I'd seen more than ten years earlier during my NDE turned out to be my biological father.[4]

Eben Alexander had a similar experience. During his NDE, he was guided by a young woman whose beautiful, infinitely loving face impressed him profoundly, although he did not recognize her. Eben had been adopted at birth. Four months after his NDE, he received a photo from his birth family of Betsy, a sister who had died before he was born. He had been told "what a hugely kind, wonderfully caring person she had been. A person . . . who was so kind she was practically an angel." He recognized Betsy, the sister he had never known, as the beautiful young woman who had so lovingly guided him during his NDE.[5]

Crossing the Veil

The previous stories indicate the eternal nature of family bonds, even with relatives we haven't met. They suggest that the veil between this world and the next really is very thin and can be crossed in all sorts of surprising ways. For example, during her NDE Amy felt so loved that she did not want to return to this life. Her guide asked her to look to her left.

As I did I saw a school bus pull up in the distance. A small child was escorted out and brought to me. I recognized that it was my own daughter, who at the time was only four years old. She had been asked in her sleep to come in spirit to help me. She walked up to me, tugged at me a little and sweetly said in an encouraging voice, "But Mommy? Who will take care of us?" . . . there was no way I could have turned down my own daughter's plea. Without hesitation, I answered, "Oh honey . . . I will, of course." My daughter was then escorted back to the bus.[6]

While Amy's experience involves a person who is having an NDE and a living person, the following story involves someone who is having an NDE and a dying person:

I was terribly ill and near death with heart problems at the same time that my sister was near death with a diabetic coma in another part of the same hospital. I left my body and went into the corner of the room, where I watched them work on me down below.

Suddenly, I found myself in conversation with my sister, who was up there with me. I was very attached to her, and we were having a great conversation about what was going on down there when she began to move away from me.

I tried to go with her, but she kept telling me to stay where I was. "It's not your time," she said. "You can't go with me because it's not your time." Then she just began to recede off into the distance through a tunnel while I was left there alone.

When I awoke, I told the doctor that my sister had died. He denied it, but at my insistence, he had a nurse check on it. She had in fact died, just as I knew she did.[7]

Wondrous as they are, these stories don't surprise us because we have experienced such things ourselves. One of several examples from my (Denny's) family is when my father was hospitalized in Minneapolis. I had been told that he was doing well, but I wanted to see him anyway. However, as Sheila and I boarded a plane in Cleveland, I sensed my father's presence as a kind of denseness around me. I told Sheila that I thought he had just died. When we changed planes in Detroit, I called the hospital and learned that my father had, indeed, died.

When we tell such stories to seminar groups, nearly everyone in the room can share a similar experience of connection with a family member who has passed on. For example, during a recent seminar Kaaran shared an experience with her father, who had worked on the railroad. She was driving home on what she describes as a "doubly dark, heavily rainy" night and approaching a railroad track. She saw a railroad conductor coming down the road toward her and waving a lantern to signal her to stop.

> I began slowing to a stop. I was surprised as I drove closer that he looked just like my deceased father had looked, even wearing a green plaid shirt just like Dad's favorite shirt had looked. Then, suddenly, he broke up into shards of light and became rain, disappearing altogether.

Kaaran was able to stop just before the railroad tracks. In the next instant, a train that had been hidden from view by some parked railroad cars came speeding through the crossing. She is certain that her father saved her from a fatal accident.[8]

No doubt, Kaaran's father will be there for her when she dies. This speaks to the question most of us may be asking: Who will be there for me when I die? Knowing that those we love will be there for us can heal even our fear of death.

For example, an anesthesiologist was making hospital rounds and entered the room of a terminally ill man:

I walked over to him and could see a look of abject horror in his eyes. Before I could say anything, he said in a raspy voice, "I'm dying. I'm so scared I don't know what to do. Please help me. . . ."

When I reached down and touched the man's hand, we crossed into another dimension and into a passageway of some kind. I have no idea if I was out of body or not; we just kept flowing toward something I cannot describe. The man looked happy and he was surrounded by other presences. I think they were family members but I couldn't ask. . . .

I turned my attention away from the whole thing and right away found myself back at the bedside right next to the man's dead body.[9]

During a heart attack, Douglas experienced something similar in his NDE, with family members who had passed on:

Now while all this was happening, two hundred miles away my grandfather had a heart attack at the same time. We were both kept alive through the night, but the next morning we both had heart attacks again. At that time I had my NDE. . . .

Off in the distance to my right was what appeared to be the shadow of a large oak tree with a large group of people standing under it. As I got closer to this group I recognized the people standing in the front of the group as my grandmother, my great-uncle Glenn, my great-aunt Lala, my great-aunt Wanda, her husband Lee, a woman that was like a grandmother to my sister and me, and then a group of people that I thought I knew, but at that time I couldn't put names to their faces. I tried to speak to them, but all they would say to me is, "We're not waiting for you; go home."

Then the last thing I remember from that side was my grandfather's voice. I did not see him; I just heard his voice say, "You're the luckiest boy I know."

Then three days later I awoke in the hospital with my mother and sister standing over my bed. My mother says that my first question was about the play I was working on at the time, and my second question was about my grandfather. . . .[10]

Douglas's mother told him that while he was having a heart attack and an NDE, his grandfather had suffered a heart attack and died in a hospital two hundred miles away. Douglas's NDE assured him that his family members, including his grandfather, would be there to welcome him when it really was his time to die. Based on the reports of many NDErs, it seems we can all have this same assurance.

Healing the Fear of Death

Although I (Matt) have not had an NDE, learning about these experiences of encountering loved ones on the other side has helped me with my own fear of death. After the reported plane crashes on September 11, 2001, I was scheduled to fly on many flights on the same routes. I wanted to cancel my commitments rather than get on a plane. I realized that the only way to overcome my fear of a plane crash was to know that, if I were killed in this way, I would experience even more life in the next world. I began writing down the names of people on the other side who had always been there for me and who I knew would love me forever. With each name, I took time to remember how they had loved me in this world and would continue to love me in the next. As I took in all this love that has no end, it became stronger than my fear of dying in a plane crash. I was again eager to fly to distant cities.

Healing Process

1. Close your eyes and put your feet flat on the floor. Breathe slowly and deeply. Place your hand on your heart and

imagine that you are breathing in and out through your heart. With each breath, let your awareness grow that you are love.

2. Imagine that you have died. You have left your body and moved into a realm of light and unconditional love. You see figures of light coming closer, welcoming you. Who are they? Who do you want to see?

3. How do you feel as you see these loved ones again? How do you feel as they embrace you? Let these feelings grow in your heart as you continue to breathe slowly and deeply.

4. What do you most want to say to each of these people? What do you most want to do?

5. As you let this unfold in your imagination, continue to let whatever you feel grow in your heart as you breathe slowly and deeply.

Reflection Questions

What touched me most in this chapter is . . .

When I reflect upon this chapter in relation to my life, I feel . . . I want . . .

⤙ 7 ⤚

Meeting Loved Ones: Animals

I myself was moving forward through it (the tunnel) . . . I became aware of people as well as animals traveling with me . . . I sensed that their experience was the same as mine.[1]

. . . a 26-year-old tropical fish collector . . . "died" after a motorcycle accident.

After revival, he testified that he had swum in an otherworldly lagoon surrounded by his deceased fish.[2]

Horses and dogs were playing together and when they stopped, they seemed to stare a hole through me and then went back to playing. I was told they were checking to see if I was the person they were waiting for, that they had loved while on earth.[3]

I forgot to mention that I had seen all the pets I had as a child in heaven. Dogs and even parakeets whom I really loved.[4]

Like most parents with children, we (Denny and Sheila) have had our share of animal burial services, ranging from birds that hit our glass windows to the most recent one of Spot, our beloved and very intelligent guinea pig. Many of the burials came with the question, "What happens to Spot (or whatever animal we were burying) when he dies?"

Our friend Harrel wondered the same thing the day that the vet arrived to put down Tedi, her fifteen-year-old golden lab. Tedi was blind, deaf, and in intense physical pain. Harrel was sobbing and holding Tedi as the vet injected her. A moment later, Harrel, who is adamant that she is not a visual person, experienced herself and her dog going into the Light. She saw Tedi enter a beautiful grassy field, where she was jumping and playing with the other dogs. Her golden hair was waving in the wind. Tedi communicated to Harrel how happy she was to be free. Harrel felt a great sense of relief that Tedi was happy and well. She wondered, "Why was I so hesitant to have Tedi put down?" Although she grieved Tedi's loss, she said that it was very different from the grief you would expect if you had just put your dog down. Her experience with Tedi has helped Harrel bring comfort to those making the painful decision to let go of their pet, as well as to those grieving their pet's death.

At important times, Tedi returns to comfort Harrel. For example, four days after putting Tedi down, Harrel's husband, Jerry, was in critical condition in the hospital ICU unit. That night, Harrel woke up crying with concern about Jerry. Tedi came to her and said, "Put your face in my fur. Put your arms around me." Unexpected as this was, it was just what Harrel needed.

Like Harrel, many people have had shared death experiences in which they accompanied their pets on their journey to the other side. For example, Karen was holding her cat, Strawberry Shortcake, when the cat died:

> I saw her ghost or spirit lift out of her body. . . . As her spirit left her body, a sort of clear doorway opened up over my left shoulder about three feet away. There were two "people" (also clear) there who opened the doorway. They were smiling and seemed happy. It seemed bright beyond the doorway. I perceived sunlight beyond it and a lot of activity. . . . There was a big popping sound, and she and the doorway disappeared.[5]

Animals on the Other Side

Like Harrel and Karen, many NDErs experience animals and deceased pets on the other side. For example, Lloyd had an NDE during a heart attack. He was surprised to see his younger brother, who had died years before. Even more surprising, "On my brother's shoulder is a bird. I look closer and it is my bird, Doolittle the parakeet. I can't take my eyes off Doolittle, and I want to ask someone why Doolittle is on my brother's shoulder." Lloyd had seen Doolittle only minutes before, and the bird was very much alive then. After Lloyd was well enough to leave the hospital, he and his wife were on their way home. He asked if Doolittle was there, and his wife said no. "My wife then tells me that Doolittle died for no apparent reason the day I had my heart attack. He died while the paramedics were working on me."[6]

Although Lloyd's experience is especially impressive because there is no way he could have known that Doolittle had died within minutes of his own heart attack, the fact that he met his beloved pet on the other side is not unique. According to P. M. H. Atwater, NDErs may be met by

> Animals and deceased pets, along with sensations of being licked, rubbed, pawed, or nosed by the animal. If not a pet, children almost invariably are greeted by smaller animals such as birds,

*chickens, bunnies, etc.; with adults, it is usually the larger ani-
mals like horses and lions. Critters sometimes converse telepathically or serve as guides.*[7]

Jan Price had such an experience during her NDE. The first
one to welcome her was her beloved springer spaniel, Maggie,
who had died several months previously. Maggie became Jan's
guide on the other side. For instance, Maggie taught Jan how to
shape forms out of energy by "pressing with your mind."[8, 9, *] We
aren't sure how you do that, but one of the places Jan visited
with Maggie was the home that Maggie had pressed for herself with her mind. Maggie's home felt welcoming—a fire in the
fireplace, an oriental rug on the floor, and beautiful paintings
on one wall. Another wall had books, and another was made
of glass and looked out onto the rolling hills, complete with a
bubbling stream.

Seated together on a love seat, Maggie draped her paws
across Jan's lap while Jan stroked Maggie's head. Sometimes
they communicated telepathically, but mainly they took in the
love between them. Eventually, Maggie continued with Jan
the tour of the other side. Finally, when it was time for Jan
to return, as she approached her physical form, Jan reported,
"Maggie was still with me, and the last thing I remember seeing
was her sweet face."[10]

One aspect of Jan's story that impresses us is how real Maggie
was to Jan's senses of sight, touch, etc. Bryce describes something similar. During a severe allergic reaction, he was clinically
dead for ten minutes. He describes his NDE as follows:

*I hear a bark, and racing toward me is a dog I once had, a
black poodle named Pepe. When I see him, I feel an emotional*

---

* P. M. H. Atwater and Nancy Danison have described being able to create things at will
during their NDEs in a way that sounds like what Jan Price learned from Maggie about
"pressing with your mind." This appears to be a creative power that we all have. See
endnote #9.

floodgate open. Tears fill my eyes. He jumps into my arms, licking my face. As I hold him, he is real, more real than I had ever experienced him. I can smell him, feel him, hear his breathing, and sense his great joy at being with me again. . . . Then I hear barking, and other dogs appear, dogs I once had. As I stand there for what seems to be an eternity, I want to embrace and be absorbed and merge. I want to stay.

In addition to his dogs, Bryce was also welcomed by his relatives who had passed on.[11]

As in the stories of Jan and Maggie or Bryce and Pepe, the people and pets we meet on the other side share many characteristics. One of them is that they both appear healthy and well. For example, when Janine saw her cat, Patty, who had suffered an agonizing death from cardiomyopathy, she was surprised that her cat appeared to be "sweet and healthy" and "three or four years old, just as she was in her prime of life." Janine felt the same surprise when she saw Lee, her teenage nephew, who had died from crippling cerebral palsy. She found herself talking to a healthy, charming young man, who she suddenly recognized. She blurted out, "My God, you're Lee." Smiling, Lee said, "Things are a lot different over here."[12, **]

Animals Care for Us From the Other Side

Like human loved ones, animals on the other side, now in their prime of life, appear fit and ready to care for us. Consider the following story of a collie named Fritz:

** Eben Alexander and Ptolemy Tompkins describe this difference. In the next world, they write, "we take on once again the entire life that we lived linearly down here, all at once. And what that produces, when someone else, another soul, sees it, is that person at their absolute, glowing best. If a person has lived a long time, they might appear physically in the full glow of their youthful beauty, but at the same time they'll be manifesting the wisdom of their later years. The people we are in the world above this one are multidimensional beings: beings who contain all the best of what they were here on earth *at the same time.*" *The Map of Heaven* (New York: Simon & Schuster, 2014),114.

Ten-year-old twins Hans and Herbert Willner of Hamburg, Germany were swimming in Lake Constance near the Austrian border when they began to have difficulty way out in the icy water more than 30 feet deep. As they started to flounder, the father, Dietrich, began to go out in the lake after them.

Suddenly, in front of a dozen eyewitnesses, the family's beloved collie Fritz, which had been dead for nearly a year, appeared by the boys. "He brought them all the way to the beach and dropped them off," Dietrich said. "While we were tending to them he just disappeared—he didn't run off, he just disappeared."[13]

Sometimes the animals that come from the other side to protect us are known to us, such as the collie, Fritz. At other times, they seem to be complete strangers. For example, Laura, just thirteen years old, was failing in school. She had been repeatedly raped and beaten, and she had no hope for her life. She was so upset one day that she fell down five flights of stairs in her apartment building. Then she heard a clicking sound, and a German shepherd "as white as snow" appeared to her. Telepathically the shepherd told her that she no longer needed to live in constant fear, and that from then on she would be watched over. Laura called the visitor "Space Dog," and from then on her life completely changed. The abuse stopped, because people "seemed to come out of the woodwork" whenever she needed protection. She stopped failing in school as her mind was flooded with new ideas day and night. Laura summarized her gratitude for Space Dog:

I am just a little four-foot, ten-inch Puerto Rican woman. Ever since Space Dog, I've had visions and they come true. I'm not trying to impress anyone, and I have nothing to gain by making this up. It happened.[14]

Whether NDErs report stories of interacting with people or with animals on the other side, the message is the same: We are all one, we are all light, and we are all in this together:

I then called my dogs and together we started walking toward the light. All colors were in the light and it was warm, a living thing, and there were people as far as the eye could see, and they were glowing with an inner light—just like my dogs. In the distance I could see fields, hills and a sky.[15]

Healing Process

1. Close your eyes and put your feet flat on the floor. Breathe slowly and deeply. Place your hand on your heart and imagine that you are breathing in and out through your heart. With each breath, let your awareness grow that you are love.

2. Recall a pet that you dearly loved. If you did not have a pet, recall any encounter with an animal that touched your heart. Get in touch with your feelings of love and appreciation for that animal, and invite it to be with you now. What is it that you most want to say and do with each other?

3. Ask the animal how it might want to care for you and accompany you, and what gift it has for you.

4. Listen for whatever comes.

Reflection Questions

What touched me most in this chapter is . . .

When I reflect upon this chapter in relation to my life, I feel . . . I want . . .

⪑ 8 ⪐

The Light

Swift as an arrow, I fly through a dark tunnel. I'm engulfed by an overwhelming feeling of peace and bliss. I feel intensely satisfied, happy, calm, and peaceful. I hear wonderful music. I see beautiful colors and gorgeous flowers in all colors of the rainbow in a large meadow. At the far end is a beautiful, clear, warm light. This is where I must go. I see a figure in a light garment. This figure is waiting for me and reaches out her hand. It feels like a warm and loving welcome. Hand in hand, we move toward the beautiful and warm light.[1]

[As her mother was dying,] Pam went to the window to adjust the blinds to detour the sun that was coming into the room. The more she messed with them, the more she realized it wasn't coming from the sun, for the sun was setting. The darker it got outside, the brighter it seemed to get in the room. She saw what looked like an arch of light; she hit the call button for the nurse to come. When she did, it was obvious that the nurse saw the same thing.

She then called other nurses in (four others, to be exact). They all witnessed this arch of bright light that began at the foot of her mom's bed and seemed to create a doorway. In order to enter the room and exit, one passed through this light. Pam took pictures with her cell phone, though they showed nothing out of the ordinary. All those present tried to touch the light, but it seemed to make no difference; it lasted close to 45 minutes. Her mother passed away shortly after, around dusk.[2]

Pam's experience of seeing an entranceway of light as her mother was dying is also reported by others. For example:

[As we sat by my mother's bedside,] suddenly, a bright light appeared in the room. My first thought was that a reflection was shining through the window from a vehicle passing by outside. Even as I thought that, however, I knew it wasn't true, because this was not any kind of light on this earth. I nudged my sister to see if she saw it too, and when I looked at her, her eyes were as big as saucers. At the same time I saw my brother literally gasp. Everyone saw it together and for a little while we were frightened.

Then my mother just expired and we all kind of breathed a big sigh of relief. At that moment, we saw vivid bright lights that seemed to gather around and shape up into . . . I don't know what to call it except an entranceway. The lights looked a bit like clouds, but that is only a comparison. We saw my mother lift up out of her body and go through that entranceway. Being by the entranceway, incidentally, was a feeling of complete joy. My brother called it a chorus of joyful feelings, and my sister heard beautiful music, although none of the rest of us did.[3]

Books on near-death experiences are abundant and varied. If we were to list their titles, we think the most common word would be "Light." If we were to reproduce their covers, we think the most common image would be a beautiful white Light that appears to come from another realm and shine down toward the reader. Phrases like "going to the Light," "returning to the Light," "healed by the Light," and so forth have become nearly synonymous with near-death experiences and with dying. The Light seems to be a universal symbol of the realm beyond our earthly life.

What Is the Light?

Most NDErs identify what they see as simply the Light. They described it as more than just brightness; NDErs and shared death experiencers consistently describe it as infinitely and unconditionally loving. Some identify it as higher beings or as a religious figure, generally consistent with their own religious tradition. Cross-cultural research on NDEs indicates that pre-existing religious beliefs may color the experience, or at least one's interpretation of it. As Elisabeth Kubler-Ross put it, "I never encountered a Protestant child who saw the Virgin Mary in his last minutes, yet she was perceived by many Catholic children."[4]

This coloring of how an NDE is interpreted includes how one identifies the Light, perhaps because in all major religions, light or beings of light are central to the sacred. Mellen-Thomas Benedict describes this tendency to identify the Light with familiar religious figures as follows:

> The Light kept changing into different figures, like Jesus, Buddha, Krishna, mandalas, archetypal images and signs. I asked the Light, "What is going on here? Please, Light, clarify yourself for me. I really want to know the reality of the situation."
> . . . The Light responded. The information transferred to me [telepathically] was that during your life after death experience, your beliefs shape the kind of feedback you are getting before the Light. If you were a Buddhist or Catholic or Fundamentalist, you

get a feedback loop of your own stuff. You have a chance to look at it and examine it, but most people do not.[5,*]

In the more complete NDEs, experiencers tend to arrive at the awareness that the Light is not a separate being, but rather it is who they really are. In Mellen-Thomas's NDE,

> *. . . the light turned into the most beautiful thing that I have ever seen: a mandala of the human souls on this planet. . . . I just went into it and, it was just overwhelming. It was like all the love you've ever wanted, and it was the kind of love that cures, heals, regenerates.*[6]

Consistent with Mellen-Thomas's experience, following is an account of the shared death experience of two sisters at their dying father's bedside, in which they saw the Light as his essence:

> *. . . a "brilliant light" filled the room. The sisters became both frightened and hopeful, since the bright light also caused their father to stir slightly. A few minutes later, though, their father stopped breathing and died.*
>
> *"The light stayed for maybe ten minutes after he died. . . . We saw no forms or figures in the light, but it seemed to be alive and have a personal presence."*

---

* In his study of over three hundred NDEs, British physician Peter Fenwick concluded that, "For a few people, the NDE is a confirmation of a religious faith they already have. But for many, perhaps most, it is a spiritual awakening that may have very little to do with religion in the narrowest sense, and nothing to do with dogma. It seems to broaden religious faith rather than simply confirm it, leading to a recognition that many paths lead to the same truth. It certainly tends to confirm belief in some form of afterlife. But there is very seldom any sense of exclusivity in the experiences: when the presence of some higher 'being' is felt, this is only seldom defined as, for example, a Catholic or Jewish God." Chris Carter, *Science and the Near-Death Experience: How Consciousness Survives Death* (Rochester, VT: Inner Traditions, 2010), 124. See also Kenneth Ring, *Heading Toward Omega* (New York, William Morrow, 1985), 143–164, 316–317.

*It was this personal presence that made them think that the light
consisted of their father's "essence," said the sisters.*[7]

Kyle Crafton describes discovering this about himself during
his NDE:

*Way off in the distance, a pinpoint of white light, and it was so
subtle it was coming toward me, and I didn't even know it until
I was completely enveloped in that light. And then I realized that
the same type of light was coming from me. I really was light.*[8]

Finally, Anita Moorjani describes her realization that she is
the Light:

*Realizing that the Light, the magnificent Universal energy is
within us and is us, changes us. . . . I could refer to it as God,
or Source, or Brahman, or All That Is, but . . . I don't perceive
the Divine as a separate entity from myself or anyone else. . . .
It transcends duality so that I'm permanently united from within
and am indivisible from it.*[9]

No Shadows

What is common in these efforts to describe the Light is a perception of infinite, unconditional love, and the realization that
this infinite, unconditional love, which manifests itself as light,
is the essence of all things, including ourselves. To understand
this, it might help to recall that our normal experience of light is
of it coming from a source other than ourselves, such as the sun,
a fire, or a lamp. Therefore, what we see is its reflection, and if
anything comes between this light and what it shines on, we see
a shadow. However, one NDEr describes the Light of his experience as follows: "The light suffuses everything." Flying over a
landscape, he saw people and a city. "He noticed his arm as he

flew toward them, expecting to see a shadow. There was none, for light shone everywhere."[10] In other words, this Light is not reflected and therefore nothing can come between to create a shadow. This Light comes from within, and it is the essence of all things. This is what Mellen-Thomas understood when he asked the being of Light, "Are you god?" The response he heard was, "Who and what is not god?"[11]

Since the Light, which is love, is the essence of all things, NDErs may return with a heightened awareness of the Light that results in an ability to see this Light vibrating in the material world around them. For example, after her NDE, Amy reported,

> . . . I could see light in and around everything. I could also see into the realm that is around ours. I could see and feel the vibration of everything around me. All of my senses were much stronger. . . . [This vibration] . . . was all around me and in everything. . . . I sensed vibrational and frequency boundaries. . . . I could even see at a cellular level. I could see something as inanimate as a chair or curtain vibrating.[12]

Another NDEr put it this way: "I often see halos around people. I am often told that I glow."[13] Yet another one said, "I could see light in all my own cells and in the universe."[14]

All Matter Is Light

These NDErs' perception of light in the material world around them is consistent with scientific research demonstrating that not only the cells of our body, but all matter is made of light. Until about one hundred years ago, the most common understanding of the basic building blocks of matter came from Newtonian physics, which described the smallest particles in terms of atoms made up of protons, neutrons, and electrons. Now, quantum physicists have discovered that the fundamental building block of nature is light; according to the physicist David Bohm, all matter is frozen light.[15]

The Gifts of Near-Death Experiences

Recent scientific research has demonstrated that bio-photons exist in the DNA of every living cell, and that they emit light. As one NDEr perceived it: "The body is the most magnificent light being there is. The body is a universe of incredible light."[16] Following is an example of this involving a drowning child, recounted by Raymond Moody:

> One fascinating patient actually luminesced—glowed— according to her father. He had to free-dive forty feet deep in Puget Sound to save her. He said he was able to find her only because she was bathed in this white light.[17]

Although we may think in terms of our own body and speak of "our" bio-photons, it is impossible to detect where our light stops and another's begins. In fact, when I communicate with you, not only are the bio-photons that comprise my light communicating with the bio-photons that comprise your light, but my bio-photons are also able to communicate with all other bio-photons in the universe, as well as with the photons in all non-living things, whether they are a few feet or trillions of miles apart. And, they communicate instantaneously.[18] That is to say, all light is connected; there is only one Light, and we are that Light.

Bookends: Two Stories Come Together in the Light

Our generation is the first to have studied two stories of Light in depth: where we came from (the "new story of the universe") and where we are going (near-death experiences). Earlier, in Chapter 3, we introduced the new story of the universe, which describes our 13.8-billion-year evolutionary journey from the original "great radiance" or explosion of light to the present. It is a story of the Light that is us. As Mellen-Thomas Benedict learned during his NDE, when he went back to the Great Radiance and even beyond, the Light is "a super-ancient part of ourselves."[19] In the great radiance, everything was one and everything was connected. Despite the apparently infinite variety of the things we see around us, it's all an expression of the same original Light. Because we are this Light, we formed the stars, the elements and the earth, just as we formed a full-grown human being from our beginning as a sperm and an egg. Our Light is endlessly creative, having already made a person and a universe.

The story of our origins is a story of our Light. The story of our destiny, as suggested by near-death experiences, is also a story of our Light.

A Window into Who We Are

Through the process of evolution, the universe developed in countless varied ways, but ultimately it is all Light. Near-death experiences remind us that we are this infinitely loving and creative Light. Most of us forget this during our life on earth. Catching the benign virus of the NDE means remembering who we are: Light.

Since very early childhood, I (Sheila) have seen Light in all things. I do not see it as I see the light from a lamp, but rather as a radiance or luminosity. It does vibrate, although for me not nearly so visibly as in Amy's account of the aftereffects of her NDE above. Thus, I have never questioned that all the things and people around me are made of Light. However, I have not always been able to maintain contact with my essence as this Light.

I have never had an NDE myself, but once, just after I finished graduate school, I was working at a spirituality center in an area surrounded by an ancient evergreen forest. Early one evening, the sun was setting and the whole scene was suffused with white, gold, and rose pink light. Everything radiated or vibrated even more intensely than I normally perceive it. At that moment, I was acutely aware of myself as the Light that constituted all the things I saw around me. Perhaps this was something of a near-death-like-experience. Gradually, an abiding sense of myself as the Light has grown within me, especially recently, as I have exposed myself to NDEs and their message has taken deep root within me. The sense of myself as Light that I had by the forest is now nearly constant. I know myself to be the Light I have always seen in all the things around me. I can no longer accept self-perceptions or cultural and religious teachings that would tell me otherwise.

I (Dennis) have never experienced the Light radiating from all things around me as Sheila has. But I did have an experience of coming in contact with my Light that changed my life. Many years ago, I was in an environment of intense love with several thousand other people. I think that because of the intensity of love around me, I, like Sheila, may have had a near-death-like-experience. What I recall is that the moments of hurt throughout my life, beginning with my earliest memories, were filled with Light. I was there for two hours, and when I left, I felt grounded and centered in myself, with an ability to connect to others that I had never previously experienced. I was so moved by the change in myself that, even though I had never written anything longer than ten pages before, I set out to write a book about that experience and the transformation within me that came from remembering my Light.

Now, some twenty books later, light remains a prominent theme in our work and in my life. Whenever I come to a stuck place in writing or in life, I still go back and fill that stuck place with Light. I now believe that those two hours I spent enveloped in intensely loving Light were so healing because they allowed me to remember the truth: I am filled with Light. That day my identity changed from being a hurt person to being one who is filled with Light. This was a great step in a journey that ultimately led to knowing that I *am* this Light. (See Chapter 18.)

If we had to summarize all our work with people in seminars and other forms of pastoral ministry, we wonder if it would come down to helping them heal the ways they have forgotten that they are Light.[20] Kenneth Ring expresses what we want for ourselves, our (Denny and Sheila's) child, and everyone else:

. . . There is an essential teaching from the Light that, NDErs say, applies to everyone. . . . It wants you to realize that your core being is this Light—it is not something external to you.[21]

Healing Process

1. Close your eyes and put your feet flat on the floor. Breathe slowly and deeply. Place your hand on your heart and imagine that you are breathing in and out through your heart.

2. Let your awareness move down to your core or essence, to the most ancient part of yourself. Imagine a tiny point of Light, glowing brightly in the depth of your being.

3. As you continue to breathe deeply in and out through your heart, watch the light grow, bigger and brighter. Despite its brightness, the Light is soft and warm.

    Let the Light continue to grow and expand within you, until it fills your whole body and extends beyond you. Let it radiate out from you until it fills all the space around you and extends as far as you can imagine.

4. Be aware that this is your Light, one with all the Light in the universe and yet unique to you. Notice any special qualities of this Light, and notice how you feel as you experience it.

5. Imagine if you really knew that you are this Light. How would you live differently each day? How would this affect your children or other loved ones?

Reflection Questions

What touched me most in this chapter is . . .

When I reflect upon this chapter in relation to my life, I feel . . . I want . . .

≈ 9 ≈

Affirming Love and Self-Esteem

In Betty Eadie's account of her NDE, she says,

Then I saw a beautiful rose that was opening and swinging to my delight and [to] the melody it created. . . . And I wanted to become a part of that rose, to feel a part of it. And somehow, I don't know how, but I was able to enter into that rose and become a part of it. But as the rose opened up and became a part of the love I had for it, it grew from my love for it. And that is how we are as human beings. We grow from the love we receive from other people.[1]

Knowing we are the infinitely loving Light of an NDE is an ideal and seemingly exalted state of self-awareness. Like all higher states of awareness, it rests upon healthy psychological development, in this case, the development of self-esteem. Self-esteem, in turn, rests upon affirming love. Ideally, we receive affirming love throughout life, initially from our parents and other caregivers and later also from other people to whom we entrust ourselves. Not surprisingly, NDEs typically include an immersion in affirming love, and the love the NDEr receives results in greatly enhanced self-esteem.

In her research on the aftereffects of NDEs, Cherie Sutherland concluded that "one of the strongest findings of this research with respect to personality changes is that after their experience, NDErs like themselves more."[2] For example, Moira said,

> At the time of my experience I believed I was a nothing, that everybody else was far better educated than I. I was a very shy person in those days . . . very diffident about my own skills. I had no skills really. I felt as if I was a downtrodden and underneath sort of person in those days, but I guess that was the way I'd been brought up. . . . But since then absolutely my whole life has changed. It's opened up and I've become more assertive and more aware of who I am.[3]

Like Moira, over 80 percent of NDErs report a dramatic increase in their self-esteem.[4] This in turn allows them to be "less dependent on the approval of others, better at dealing with stress, and more adventurous, and they also take greater risks. It changes people's attitudes toward their body and alerts them to new ways of thinking."[5]

Affirming Love Heals

These changes are the result of feeling loved unconditionally for oneself. Ned, for example, was not proud of his life. He owned a nightclub and the evening of his NDE, he almost strangled a business associate to death during a fight. Then Ned had a heart attack. During the NDE that followed, he found himself in a huge, glowing amphitheater filled with thousands of spiritual beings who were

> . . . communicating, by musical sounds, feelings of good will to me. Their sounds of greeting were in harmony with the symphonic sounds of energy emanating from the amphitheater. . . .

I was overwhelmed by the awesome sight before me, but the feelings of love that were conveyed to me by the spiritual beings were even more overwhelming. The spiritual beings were cheering me, conveying loving encouragement and support. "You are doing wonderfully. We are here to support you. Continue to do good work, and we will help you. You are part of us, and we are part of you."[6]

Ned found this difficult to accept at first. He regarded his actions during his life as hardly wonderful. Yet, he understood that he was loved for himself, and he was able to take in that love.

Like Ned in the amphitheater in the midst of thousands of cheering beings, during his life review, Andy Petro experienced being loved for himself. He found himself surrounded by billions and billions of lights, and he was astounded that each light loved him personally and called him by name. They told him, "Welcome home, Andy. We love you." Andy responded, "I'm home. I'm home, at last, I'm home."[7] Being loved unconditionally for oneself, for no other reason than simply because one exists, is in our experience the foundation of self-esteem. Self-esteem is, in turn, the foundation of psychological healing and health. We speak of the kind of love that lays this foundation as "affirming love," because it affirms the essential goodness of the person.

In the introduction, we mentioned the women's prison in Massachusetts where we met Ellie. That first time we went to give a program for the residents, we did a process with the group of about thirty women who attended. We asked for a volunteer to help us, and Marsha raised her hand. We invited her to sit in front of the rest of the group. Then we encouraged all the rest of the women to express their love and appreciation for Marsha.

These women know why each one is in prison. Regardless of the charges that got them sent there, their real "crime" is to devalue themselves and let themselves be degraded. They learned early to treat themselves in this way, since nearly all female prisoners were sexually abused as children or as young women.

Whatever the reasons they are in prison, these women live closely together and know each other's weaknesses very well. Yet, no one had any difficulty thinking of something affirming to say to Marsha about why they appreciated her. Although some of the women spoke of kind things Marsha had done, their comments were mostly about the essential goodness they saw in her. They loved her simply because she was Marsha. What stands out in our memory is the change in Marsha as she listened. Her posture straightened, her sallow skin grew pink, and she literally glowed. She had remembered her Light. We wrote down all the comments and gave them to Marsha to keep so that she could remind herself.

The Light Affirms Us

The process we did with Marsha at the prison is one we often do in many situations: at baptisms, weddings, birthday parties, family celebrations on holidays, and so forth. When we celebrate a wedding, we invite all the guests to light a candle and share something they love about the bride or the groom. At a birthday party, we ask everyone present to tell the one whose birthday we are celebrating why they are glad he or she was born. We do this not only at seminars and celebrations, but we also try to make it a way of life. For example, when we write Christmas cards, we include something we appreciate about each person to whom we are writing.

In all these ways we are trying to give others the experience of seeing their goodness reflected back to them in the eyes of someone who loves them. We now realize that this is a limited, earthly version of being beheld by the Light during an NDE and seen in all the beauty of one's true self. For example, the core of Anita Moorjani's NDE and the aspect of it that she experienced as healing her of cancer was being "filled with the knowledge that I was simply magnificent!" (See Chapter 16.) She describes how this happened:

> I still felt myself completely enveloped in a sea of unconditional love and acceptance. I was able to look at myself with fresh eyes, and I saw that I was a beautiful being of the Universe. I understood that just the fact that I existed made me worthy of this tender regard rather than judgment. I didn't need to do anything specific; I deserved to be loved simply because I existed, nothing more and nothing less.
>
> This was a rather surprising realization for me, because I'd always thought I needed to work at being lovable. I believed that I somehow had to be deserving and worthy of being cared for, so it was incredible to realize this wasn't the case. I'm loved unconditionally, for no other reason than simply because I exist.[8]

We all need to know what Anita experienced: that we are loved simply because we exist. Following are two processes, the first to help us experience this for ourselves and the second to share it with another.

Healing Process for Oneself

1. Close your eyes and put your feet flat on the floor. Breathe slowly and deeply. Place your hand on your heart and imagine that you are breathing in and out through your heart.

2. Recall a moment when you felt connected to your true self and good about who you are.

3. Imagine that you have died and you are in the presence of the Light. The Light sees you completely, perfectly, and in every aspect of your being. Nothing is hidden, including the parts of yourself that you regard as faults and weaknesses and the things you have done that you now regret. However,

none of this matters to the Light in comparison with the infinite and utter goodness of your true self, the self you have had a glimpse of in your best moments.

4. Breathe in the affirming love you feel in the presence of the Light, knowing that you are loved infinitely, simply because you exist as the uniquely wonderful person that you are.

Healing Process with Another

1. Recall the healing process for yourself, above, and experience again being infinitely loved by the Light. Rest in knowing the depth of your goodness as your unique self.

2. You are one with the Light. As the Light that you are, notice the goodness in the person you are with. Perhaps you notice the kindness in his eyes, the warmth of her smile, the firm steadiness in his posture, the honesty in her words, and so forth.

3. Let the goodness you notice move your heart so that you feel delight in what you perceive, and especially in the other person.

4. Express your delight in some way, perhaps by letting your appreciation for this person shine from your eyes, perhaps by using words to express it, perhaps by reaching out with an embrace . . . whatever feels right to you.

Reflection Questions

What touched me most in this chapter is . . .

When I reflect upon this chapter in relation to my life, I feel . . . I want . . .

Prologue to the Life Review

There is never any condemnation—you are not judged.
You are in the presence of a being who loves you unconditionally.
You are treated with total compassion.
You are already forgiven.
You are only asked to look at your life, and to understand.

—Kenneth Ring, *Lessons from the Light*, 164

These words set the tone for the element of an NDE known as the life review. The following three chapters address three aspects of life that may be included in a life review: memories of love, how we have been hurt, and how we have hurt others. The first of these chapters is on memories of love, because we need the foundation of love and the self-esteem to which it gives rise in order to face how we have been hurt and how we have hurt others.

Following are two accounts of life reviews that include elements of what will be discussed in the following chapters. The first is from the NDE of a young boy who, like many people, fears that he will be judged but learns otherwise:

Then I started to see this movie of my life. I somehow knew I was being judged or something and I remember thinking, "How

bad can this be I'm only eight years old?" I was wrong. He was
showing me things with a lovely smile. I knew I was in trouble.
He showed me the time I scratched my neighbor's car with a key;
I could feel how bad this man felt. I was thinking, how many
points for that bad thing. My angel knew what I was thinking
about and said, "Don't worry, that was just a lesson." He then
told me, "It's the things that I do out of love that count."[1]

The second account is of a shared life review as described
by Dana:

It was on my husband Johnny's fifty-fifth birthday when the doc-
tor told us that Johnny had lung cancer and had maybe about six
months to live. . . .

From that day until Johnny died, we weren't separated from each
other more than a few hours. I was beside him the whole time in
the hospital and was holding onto him when he died. When he
did, he went right through my body. It felt like an electric sensa-
tion, like when you get your finger in the electrical socket, only
much more gentle.

Anyway, when that happened our whole life sprang up around us
and just kind of swallowed up the hospital room and everything in
it in an instant. There was light all around. . . . Everything we
ever did was in that light. . . .

Dana saw Johnny as a teenager, behaving in ways that ordi-
narily might have been upsetting to her. But in this shared life
review, they were not. She saw him with classmates, and

. . . later I searched for them in his high school yearbook and was
able to find them, just based on what I saw during the life review
during his death.

In the middle of this life review, I saw myself there holding onto his dead body, which didn't make me feel bad because he was also completely alive, right beside me, viewing our life together. By the way, the life review was like a "wraparound." I don't know how else to describe it. It was a wraparound scene of everything Johnny and I experienced together or apart. There is no way I could even put it into words other than to say that all of this was in a flash, right there at the bedside where my husband died.

Then, right in the middle of this review, the child that we lost to a miscarriage when I was still a teenager stepped forth and embraced us. She was not a figure of a person exactly as you would see a human being, but more the outline or sweet, loving presence of a little girl. The upshot of her being there was that any issues we ever had regarding her loss were made whole and resolved. I was reminded of the verse from the Bible about "the peace that passeth all understanding." That's how I felt when she was there.

One of the funny things about this wraparound view of our life was that we had gone to Atlanta in the seventh grade, to the state capitol, where there was a diorama. So at one point we were watching this wraparound and watching ourselves in another wraparound—a diorama—where we stood side by side as kids. I burst out laughing and Johnny laughed too, right there beside me.[2]

⤚ 10 ⤙

Life Review: Memories of Love

In an instant, I was seeing my life in review—first all of the wonderful feelings that brought joy into my life. I saw all of the incredible events of my life when love . . . was most present. . . . Childhood memories, my first real loves, the births of my children, the first time I knew I loved my wife more than I loved myself. I saw anything and everything associated with love . . . flying past my eyes and filling my heart with a joy that felt almost overwhelming in its scope.[1]

One of the most well-known aspects of a near-death experience is the "life review," experienced by up to about one-fourth of NDErs.[2] An NDE is not the only way to recall memories of love. The overwhelming joy the NDEr quoted above felt in seeing all the "incredible events" of his life "when love was most present" reminds us of the joy our (Denny and Sheila's) son experiences when he looks at his photo albums. Every year on his birthday, I (Sheila) create a photo album of the past year's events that seemed to touch John's heart most. He is now seventeen, and so he has seventeen albums. One of John's favorite things to do when he has friends over is to share his albums with them and take them on a journey of the "incredible events of his life when love was most present." The joy he expresses at these times encourages me to create next year's album—his eighteenth life review.

Being in the Movie

The life review is sometimes thought of as looking at a photo album, as John does, or as watching your life flash before you, as if on a movie screen. From the descriptions of those who have experienced it, the life review is often more like being in the movie and experiencing it from the point of view of every one of the characters. The NDEr feels the feelings of each person with whom she interacted during life and understands her effect on all those people: "You are given insight into the impact of your thoughts, words, and deeds on yourself and others. So it appears that every thought we have is a form of energy that continues to exist forever."[3]

The lesson of the life review is that nothing is ever lost. As Justin experienced during his NDE,

> I went to the light which was . . . pure unconditional love and acceptance. . . . At that time I then experienced a partial life review.
>
> Many events in my life I experienced, but not from how I remembered it but from . . . how the people, animals, environment experienced it around me. . . . The times I had made others happy, and sad, I felt it all as they did. It was very apparent that every single thought, word, and action affects everything around us and indeed the entire universe. Trees, plants, animals, too.[4]

Random Acts of Kindness

Most of us worry that we will be held accountable for the things we have done of which we are ashamed. However, often, it is our goodness that we hide even more than our faults and mistakes. For example, two sisters shared the life review of their dying mother:

> The sisters were at their mother's bedside as she was dying of lung cancer. As her breathing became more labored, the room began to "light up," said one of the sisters. Both of them told of how the room began to swirl, quickly at first before slowing to a stop. Then the two women found themselves standing with their mother, who looked decades younger.
>
> Together, they were immersed in their mother's life review, which was filled with many scenes they had lived and many they had not. . . . They saw small things that had meant a lot to their mother, like the times she had helped poor children at their school without telling anyone. . . .
>
> "What we saw was so real that we thought we had died too," said one of the sisters. "For months it was beyond belief until we finally accepted it."[5]

In this world, we often measure goodness in grandiose terms and attribute it to heroes or heroines, philanthropists, or other famous people. However, the "Practice Random Acts of Kindness" bumper stickers may have it right, since many NDErs say that small, spontaneous gestures of the heart are what matter most.

Erica McKenzie, who had two life reviews, experienced the importance of random acts of kindness. In her first life review, she saw all the happy events and accomplishments that were important to her, from her first tooth, to her athletic awards, to graduating from high school. In her second life review, she saw her life from the viewpoint of the Light: all her thoughts, words, and actions that were loving. In this review were none of what she had considered her accomplishments. Instead, she saw small acts of kindness, such as befriending someone who was often treated cruelly, helping an elderly person cross the street, or caring for a neglected animal.[6]

Like Erica, Reinee Pasarow experienced the importance of simple gestures of love. In her NDE, she realized that the single best thing she ever did was reach out to an unpopular boy at a summer camp because she wanted him to know that he was loved. She reported that during her life review, this act of kindness was more important from her viewpoint of expanded awareness than if she had been the president of the United States or the queen of England.[7]

Ultimately, what seems to matter most is not the outward, worldly significance of what we do, but the depth of love with which we do it. For example, as a child, Kimberly Clark Sharp

> . . . saw a tiny flower growing almost impossibly out of a crack in the sidewalk. She bent down and cupped the flower and gave it her full unconditional love and attention. When the girl became a woman and had a NDE, during her life review she discovered that it was this incident with the flower that was the most important event of her entire life. The reason was because it was the moment where she expressed her love in a greater, purer, and unconditional manner.[8]

And how did the flowers feel about this? A silly question, you might think. Yet, in his life review, Tom Sawyer re-experienced

> . . . the day when I, nine years old, walked through Seneca Park and loved the appearance of a tree. . . . I could experience a bit of what the tree experienced in my loving it, two little photons of love and adoration. It was somewhat like the leaves acknowledging my presence. Can a tree experience that? Yes, it can.[9]

Finally, here is a story of a simple, spontaneous act of kindness that saved a man's life, from a shared life review involving a man named Ted who had been a railroad worker. His friend and coworker for nearly twenty years was dying of lung cancer, and Ted came to be with him. When his friend's breathing finally stopped, Ted saw a "wispy, transparent 'something'—as formless as smoke" that arose from his friend's chest. Then, Ted said,

All of a sudden I was above my body, watching the scene below. I could feel movement, like the kind you feel when a train leaves the station and the ground shifts, or you are on one train and another next to you starts moving.

The room around us became very bright and then I started to see flashes—scenes—of all the years we had worked together on the rails.

One of the events really stood out. We were checking the boxcars one night in Illinois. It was a very cold night, so bitter cold that I had sweaters and a down jacket on and a wool cap and thick gloves and I could still hardly stand to be outside.

As we walked down the line of cars, we found a drunk drifter lying in the grass next to the train. He was not dressed very warm and wasn't responding very well to us, even though we were shaking him pretty hard to wake him up. He was obviously drunk, but also was having a problem with hypothermia. The engineer was radioing us to hurry up, but when we found that drunk we called the local police and told the engineer that we had to wait with the man until the police came to make sure he didn't freeze to death. . . . The engineer was mad as heck that we didn't just let the guy go. . . . Everyone wanted us to leave him, but we wouldn't do it. He would have frozen to death.[10]

Attuning Ourselves to Kindness

The message of these stories is that the good we do endures forever, and it ripples out in ways we cannot foresee:

> [In my life review] I saw myself perform an act of kindness, just a simple act of unselfishness, and I saw the ripples go out. . . . The friend I had been kind to was kind in turn to one of her friends, and the chain repeated itself. I saw love and happiness increase in others' lives because of that one simple act on my part. I saw their happiness grow and affect their lives in positive ways, some significantly. . . . I felt the love they felt, and I felt their joy, and this from one simple act of kindness.[11]

The importance of NDEs is not so much what they teach us about the afterlife, but rather what they can teach us about how to live now. Therefore, how can we attune ourselves to goodness and make kindness more of a habit so that we live more fully and consistently as the love that we are?

One thing that has helped us (and that we will explore further in Chapter 14) is asking ourselves at the end of every day: For what moment today am I most grateful? Then we share these moments that our (Denny and Sheila's) son, John, has called since he was two, our "favorite things" from the day. Having reflected on our experience of the day regularly in this way, we see a pattern. The pattern we notice is how often the moment for which we are most grateful is a time when we were kind to another person. This pattern is self-reinforcing, in that when we identify our favorite thing from the day, we are likely to want to do more of it.

For example, about a year ago, John's favorite moment from the day was when he ran home from school, grabbed Denny and said, "Can you give my friends a ride? They missed the bus, and they have to walk to town, and they're carrying a big bass guitar." Denny and John jumped in the car and found John's classmates only slightly closer to town than when they had started, weighed down as they were by the guitar. One of the boys is not popular, and John has often commented on how left out he must feel. When John recalled this experience that evening, he felt happy that he had helped his friends. He was especially happy that he had done something kind for a boy who needs to know that other people care about him. He felt so good about this that he was eager to find other ways to reach out to the same boy.

Another time, John's favorite moment from the day was when he helped out at the eighth birthday party of a friend who adores then-sixteen-year-old John. A couple of weeks ago, my (Denny's) favorite moment was when I spent some time listening empathically to a Hispanic single mother who is here illegally and is usually treated like a servant rather than listened to as a human being. My (Matt's) favorite moment one night last week was taking all of us to see the movie 42 (about Jackie Robinson, the first African American major league baseball player), and how much it meant to everyone. Sometimes such moments move us so deeply that we write about them, as I (Sheila) did in Chapter 2 with the story of paying the fine for the woman in the library.

These are typical examples of how often our favorite moments from the day are times when we were kind to someone else. And, because these moments give us so much joy, reflecting upon them encourages us to do them even more often. Such moments remind us of who we are and of what we most deeply want, which is to contribute to the well-being of others and of all life.

The lesson of the positive aspects of a life review in an NDE is that being "good" makes us happy. Thus, we needn't *make* ourselves be good, in the sense of forcing ourselves to extend kindness to others. Rather, if we simply notice how happy it makes us to express the love that we are, we are likely to spontaneously behave in this way more often.

We can also reflect on times when others have been kind to us and notice how those moments affect us. My (Sheila's) experience matches exactly the reports of NDErs, that it is the simplest things that matter the most. For example, when I was in sixth grade, we moved from Massachusetts to Florida for just that year. I hated it. I hated the hot, humid Florida climate. I hated the rows of pastel cookie-cutter houses in our neighborhood. I hated my new school. I hated it because I had no friends and felt so alone. On Valentine's Day, the other children exchanged cards, but I was nobody's valentine.

I somehow managed to get out of my classroom unnoticed and went to the playground. I sat alone on a swing, utterly bereft. I didn't notice him coming, but a boy from my class sat down on the swing next to mine. His name was Richard and he wore glasses. He began to swing alongside me. I don't remember if he said anything, only that he was with me and I was not alone any more. I have never forgotten him or the utter kindness of what he did for me that day. When I die, I will look for him and thank him. However, if he has had an NDE that included a life review, he already knows how much his kindness meant to me. Perhaps he will be searching for me to thank *me* for the happiness I imagine he feels about what he did.

As I feel the quality or energy of this memory, I understand the power of simple kindness, and I try to match its energy as I relate to others. Following is a process that we hope can help us all to be the goodness and love that we are.

Healing Process

1. Close your eyes and put your feet flat on the floor. Breathe slowly and deeply. Place your hand on your heart and imagine that you are breathing in and out through your heart.

2. Recall a moment when another person was kind to you in a very simple way that seemed heartfelt and that touched you deeply. Let yourself go back in your imagination to that

moment, be there again, and feel the effect upon you. Let your heart swell with gratitude or whatever else you were feeling at the time.

3. Recall moments when you have matched the energy of kindness that you have received, by reaching out to others in a similar way. Let these moments grow inside you. Find the place in yourself that deeply longs to do such things. This is the love you are, waiting and watching for ways to express itself.

Reflection Questions

What touched me most in this chapter is . . .

When I reflect upon this chapter in relation to my life, I feel . . . I want . . .

⚛ 11 ⚛

Life Review: Who Has Hurt Me?

We have all experienced hurts. Many of us spend much of our lives seeking healing of these hurts, and if we persevere we may find it to a considerable extent. In our experience, what ultimately heals life's hurts is love, and the near-death experience is a total immersion in infinite, unconditional love. Although an NDE is hardly a guarantee that all one's psychological and emotional issues will be resolved, a great deal of healing can take place in a very short time.

For example, Barbara was severely physically punished by her mother as a very young child. Like most children in such situations, she blamed herself and regarded herself as a bad person. This led to many difficulties in relating to others. Here is how she describes her healing during her NDE:

I was picking up all the physical sensations of my mother hitting me again. . . . I was saying "no wonder." No wonder you are the way you are, you know? Lookit, what's being done to you at such a young age. . . .

It was like I was understanding how insecure I was and how inferior I felt because nobody had put their arms around me and given me a sense of value. . . . Then I was able to see my whole life unwinding from that perspective of this poor, neurotic little girl. . . . I was watching this whole childhood unfold . . . so that I had a better understanding of all the rejection I had felt. . . . Everyone else was just coming from their own problems and hang-ups. All of that stuff that had been layered on me was because my vision of what was going on was really screwed up. [This life review] was like the most healing therapy there could be. . . . I was forgiving myself for not always being good. I was forgiving myself for being as neurotic as I had been.[1]

In the Light of unconditional love and understanding, Barbara was able to give herself love and understanding. We might say she walked in her own shoes, perhaps for the first time, and was reunited with her self. When we are hurt, we normally separate from ourselves in some way. We may distrust our own knowing and deny what has actually happened. We may turn against ourselves and blame ourselves. We may find the painful feelings of hurt overwhelming and cut ourselves off from them, thereby cutting ourselves off from our vital self. In all these ways, we lose contact with our essence and that, really, is the heart and core of our wounding. During her NDE, Barbara recovered her essence.

How Are Hurts Healed?

Barbara's experience of healing in her NDE is an immensely accelerated version of the process of healing hurts that we have experienced in our own lives and in our work. There are at least three critical elements in healing. All these elements are part of the life review in an NDE, but in a dramatically greater and more intense way.

First is the degree of love and rapport between the helper and the one receiving healing. This helps the receiver to feel deeply heard, understood, known, and valued as the person he or she is. Being known and valued in this way leads to an assurance of one's goodness and relieves the fear that one may have deserved to be hurt or abused. The NDEr is in an environment of perfect rapport and infinite love. The person feels seen and known as never before in life. As Barbara described it,

> . . . there was something with me that was just wonderful. It was an all-encompassing energy. Even if everything I saw would have made me out to be evil, it would have been okay. Whatever this was that was with me just loved me the way I was.[2]

A second element in healing is confidence that we can set boundaries to protect ourselves so that we will not be hurt again in the future in a similar way. These boundaries include a boundary around our authentic self, in the sense of an ability to resist messages about ourselves from the outer world that are not congruent with our essence.

In Barbara's case, she had been unable to set a boundary between her real self and her parents' view of her. Instead, she internalized their view and constructed a false sense of self around it. In an NDE, the need to set boundaries to protect oneself in the future is taken care of by the assurance that one's real core can never be violated. Thus, during Barbara's NDE, a lifetime of conditioning to see herself as her parents saw her was undone in a moment. After she returned, she was able to develop as the authentic self that had been overwhelmed and buried by her parents' conditioning.[3]

The third element in healing hurts, when we are ready, is empathy and compassion for the person who hurt us, which allows us to forgive. The life review in an NDE provides a tremendous advantage in forgiveness, because it often includes experiencing the thoughts and feelings of everyone the NDEr interacted with, including those who hurt him or her. As Barbara put it,

[I felt] a great deal of forgiveness and compassion for people that I thought were being mean to me. There was just a great deal of understanding that we had formed a bad pattern because of my defensiveness in my entire life, and I had put them into the mold they were in of treating me the way I thought they were treating me to the point where I actualized that treatment. And I could understand their beauties and their qualities. And it was like all the slates were being wiped clean. . . . It was the kind of a thing where I just wasn't the victim anymore; we had all been victims.[4]

Like good psychotherapy, the NDE includes unconditional love, safe boundaries around one's essential self, and compassion for others. Many NDErs have described the NDE as being like many years of the best therapy in just a few minutes. As Barbara put it, "Years and years of intense psychoanalysis of the most intense type of external therapy could not have brought me through what I was experiencing rapidly."[5]

Walking in Our Own Shoes

The core of Barbara's healing during her NDE was her ability to have compassion for herself, which evolved naturally into compassion for the people who had hurt her. In other words, she walked in her own shoes and only then did she walk in the shoes of others. "Nice" people—like the three of us—often push themselves to have empathy and compassion for others before they have sufficiently received those things for themselves. In our work, we sometimes did to others what we were doing to ourselves. For example, in our seminars on forgiveness, we included a "Shoe Prayer." We asked participants to get in touch with a person who had hurt them, and then we asked them to exchange right shoes with their neighbor. The right shoe was to represent the world of the person who had hurt them. They were to put on that unfamiliar shoe and imagine walking in the world of the person who hurt them as a way to grow in compassion for that person.

As the three of us go through a process of healing like Barbara's, albeit much slower than hers, we realize the need to begin with compassion for ourselves before pushing ourselves to have compassion for others. Now, during our seminars, if we include the Shoe Prayer, we encourage participants to walk in the left shoe (their own shoe) for as long as they wish before walking in the right shoe (representing the world of the person who hurt them).

An NDE Is in Fast Forward

In an NDE, the intensity of love and compassion that the NDEr receives is so intense that, as mentioned above, many years of healing can take place in a few minutes. The NDEr is overflowing with love for everyone and everything. Moreover, because the life review often gives NDErs the extra advantage of seeing their life from their own perspective and from everyone else's at the same time, NDErs typically arrive at a considerable depth of empathy and compassion for those who have hurt them. In other words, having been profoundly accompanied as they walked in their own shoes, they are able to walk in the shoes of the people who hurt them. Amy experienced this in her NDE:

> I was able to enter the minds and emotional centers of many who had been around me, and understand where they were coming from in their own thinking. . . . . I felt their own struggling and their own fears . . . their own desperate need for love and approval . . . and more than anything, I could feel how child-like everyone was. . . . And the feeling I had toward everyone was nothing less than what a loving mother would feel for her own children at toddler age. . . .
>
> . . . I was able to explore the mind or energetic pattern of one of my life's sworn enemies, someone I couldn't imagine forgiving

for what I'd witnessed. And yet, coming back from my NDE, I could feel nothing more than such a flood of love for this woman that I dived in at the chance to write her a letter and tell her how much I loved her, and to ask for forgiveness for the energetic weight I may have held over her from my own dark thoughts and anger. She could have been my own firstborn. This is how much I adored her at that time. . . . It was such a surprisingly marvelous feeling to relinquish the burden of my own anger and judgments. Much of which I hadn't even carried consciously most of my years.[6]

We suspect that, like ourselves, most of our readers have been on some sort of journey of healing and personal growth. We have been peeling away the layers of hurts and defenses and adaptations to the expectations of other people and our culture as a whole. We have been searching for our essence, which is unconditional love. Barbara and Amy each found their essence during an NDE. Although our journey may be slower, the process is similar for the rest of us, and their stories may help us trust that our essence as the Light is indestructible and is only waiting for us to reclaim it.

Healing Process

The healing of hurts that takes place in the Light during an NDE is rapid and deep, but not qualitatively different from what can happen in this life, especially when we know that all the resources of the Light are available to us. Even more, they are within us.

1. Close your eyes and put your feet flat on the floor. Breathe slowly and deeply. Place your hand on your heart and imagine that you are breathing in and out through your heart.

2. Recall a moment from your life when you experienced unconditional, non-judgmental love, a moment when you knew your goodness. Hold those feelings in your heart and let them grow there.

3. Now imagine that you have died and are in the presence of the Light. It is far brighter than any light you have ever seen, but it does not hurt your eyes. The Light is alive and loving. The love you experience is at least a million times greater than the moment you just recalled, and your sense of your essential goodness is that much greater as well. Rest in this for as long as you wish, continuing to breathe in and out through your heart.

4. Now let your life review begin. First recall moments when you were kind and loving to others, including the natural world, such as plants or animals. Let feelings of appreciation for yourself grow in your heart, as you continue to breathe deeply.

5. Now get in touch with a way you have been hurt that still affects you. As you recall what happened, notice what you feel in your body. Where in your body do you still carry the feelings associated with this hurt? Put your hand on this place now, in a caring way, as you would put your hand on a hurting child.

6. Become aware that you are the Light and that you are unconditional love. Be that loving Light for yourself now, as you ask this place to tell you the story of how it feels and what it needs. Do this for as long as it takes you to feel heard and cared for. You may wish to come back and do this again many times before considering if you want to do the next steps.

7. Gently and without pushing yourself, focus your awareness on the person who hurt you. As the Light that you are, ask yourself what might have been going on within that person

to cause his or her behavior toward you. As you do so, notice any movement of empathy and compassion within yourself toward that person.

8. As far as you feel truly ready to do so, in your imagination send that empathy and compassion to the person who hurt you. If you find this difficult, return to Step 6 and stay there for as long as you wish.

Reflection Questions

What touched me most in this chapter is . . .

When I reflect upon this chapter in relation to my life, I feel . . . I want . . .

⤢ 12 ⤡

Life Review: Whom Have I Hurt?

In the previous chapter, we focused on those who have hurt us. When we have been hurt, unless we have found considerable self-awareness and healing, we pass on that hurt in some way. We may act it out against ourselves or against others. In Barbara's NDE (see the previous chapter), she experienced this cycle of hurt. As Barbara realized, in this cycle everyone is a victim and everyone needs healing in the unconditionally loving, non-judgmental Light. This is important to remember as we explore how we have hurt others.

Barbara hurt people in what we would normally consider small ways, such as by projecting her own fears of rejection onto others and by being unavailable for a real relationship because she felt so insecure. In contrast, consider the story of a former Nazi who hurt people in big ways, by killing them in concentration camps. He had an NDE while he was in a coma. The coma lasted forty-eight hours, but it seemed to him that it lasted a lifetime. He was in a dark cave with Nazi and Roman soldiers who had been responsible for mass killings. After a while, he saw a different part of the place where light was shining, and there were the people he had killed. He wanted to ask their forgiveness. He heard that he had already been forgiven, and that now he only needed to forgive himself. He felt unable do this, and so he was allowed to feel the pain and suffering he had caused each of his victims. Afterward, all these people comforted him. "He was bathed in unconditional love; it permeated his entire being." Then he awoke from his coma.[1]

Whether we have hurt others in small ways, as Barbara did, or in horrific ways, as the Nazi soldier did, our actions do have consequences, and at some point we will be asked to face whatever pain we have caused. Yet, accounts of NDEs consistently indicate that this has nothing to do with judgment or punishment. The life review takes place in an environment of infinite, unconditional love. The NDEr can ask that the life review stop temporarily if it becomes overwhelming, and she or he can rest for a while in unconditional love before going on. The reason for facing the harm we have done to others is so that we learn from our mistakes and grow in love and compassion, including compassion for ourselves.

The life review encourages us to realize that everything we do affects all other creatures. Again, nothing is lost:

> . . . the life review demonstrates that psychologically and spiritually, there is really only one person in the universe—and that person is, of course, yourself. Every act, every thought, every feeling, every emotion directed toward another—whether you know the person or not—will later be experienced by you. Everything you send out returns. . . .[2]

An NDEr named Tom Sawyer experienced this quite dramatically during his life review. As a young person, Tom had a terrible temper. One day he was driving his pickup truck and nearly hit a pedestrian. Angry that the man had almost damaged his truck, Tom got into an argument with the man, hit him thirty-two times, and left him unconscious in the street. During his life review, Tom experienced this from the point of view of his

·victim and felt every one of the thirty-two blows. Tom describes this as follows:

> *I also experienced seeing Tom Sawyer's fist come directly into my face. And I felt the indignation, the rage, the embarrassment, the frustration, the physical pain. I felt my teeth going through my lower lip—in other words, I was in that man's eyes. I was in that man's body. I experienced everything of that interrelationship between Tom Sawyer and that man that day.[3]*

Similar to Tom Sawyer's experience is that of Roland Webb. In his life review, Roland saw himself as a child outdoors with a playmate, Heidi. He decided to whack a beehive and then raced off into a building. Once inside, he held the door closed, which made it impossible for Heidi to find protection from the bees. As Roland said, "All those bees from the beehive stung the daylights out of Heidi." In his life review, Roland felt every single bee sting and the resulting swelling. He also experienced Heidi's mother's fear and rage. He said, "I felt every single thing."[4]

During an intense spiritual experience similar to an NDE, Rene Jorgensen also experienced the impact of his behavior on others:

> *I . . . went back all the way to fourth grade when I was teasing a small girl, maybe second or third grade. . . . She was up against a wall and I was calling her names. But now I was inside her body, and I was receiving my own actions. And not only was I feeling her pain, I was also seeing the future, how she as a person would become more shy and inward as a consequence to my actions. And not only that, I would also feel the pain of her parents for realizing that their child would become inward, shy, and closed as a person. So, I was basically experiencing the full consequences of my actions. . . . It was not just that I was teasing this little girl and she was shy. It was also her parents' sadness, because*

everybody has hope and love for their children. They want them to grow and bloom in life. So, I experienced the full cycle, the chain of my actions.[5]

Indirect Injuries to Others

During the life review, we experience the impact of our behavior not only on those we hurt directly and sometimes their families, as Tom, Roland, and Rene did, but also on those we hurt indirectly. As one NDEr describes it,

> I was shown the ripple effect. . . . I saw how I had often wronged people and how they had often turned to others and committed a similar wrong. This chain continued from victim to victim, like a circle of dominoes, until it came back to the start—to me, the offender.[6]

Following is another account of a life review, in which a scroll began to unroll before the eyes of a prisoner:

> . . . the only pictures on it were the pictures of people I had injured. It seemed there would be no end to it. A vast number of those people I knew or had seen. Then there were hundreds I had never seen. These were people who had been indirectly injured by me. The minute history of my long criminal career was thus relived by me, plus all the small injuries I had inflicted unconsciously by my thoughtless words and looks and omissions. Apparently nothing was omitted in this nightmare of injuries, but the most terrifying thing about it was that every pang of suffering I had caused others was now felt by me as the scroll unwound itself.[7]

Such accounts leave us wondering how our world might be different if they were read by those who foment wars and profit from them, executives of corporations that produce unhealthy food and pollute the environment, corrupt government leaders, and so forth.

Life Reviews Include the Non-Human World

Our impact on other creatures includes non-human ones. For example, during Berkley Carter Mills's NDE,

> He relived each incident in his life, including killing a mother bird when he was eight. He was so proud of that single shot until he felt the pain the bird's three babies went through when they starved to death without her. It's not true that only humans have souls," Mills cautions today. "Insects, animals, plants have souls, too. Yes, I still eat meat . . . but I bless my food and say thanks for the gift life gives. If I don't the food sours in my stomach."[8]

No matter how our actions have affected others, the purpose of the life review appears to always be healing, self-knowledge, and growth in compassion for ourselves and others, including the non-human world. Following is P. M. H. (Phyllis) Atwater's account of how she arrived at this:

> Mine was not a review, it was a reliving. For me, it was a total reliving of every thought I had ever thought, every word I had ever spoken, and every deed I had ever done; plus the effect of each thought, word, and deed on everyone and anyone who had ever come within my environment or sphere of influence whether I knew them or not (including unknown passers by on the street); plus the effect of each thought, word, and deed on weather, plants, animals, soil, trees, water, and air. . . .
>
> No detail was left out. No slip of the tongue or slur was missed. No mistake nor accident went unaccounted for. . . . It was me judging me, and my judgment was most severe . . . but I took

interest and satisfaction from one characteristic she [Phyllis] had repeatedly displayed, and that was her desire to try and try again. . . . She was relentless in her determination to make of herself a better person and to learn everything possible. . . . This pleased me and at last I pronounced her personality good and the life she had lived worth its living. . . .

As I looked down at the body of Phyllis on the floor, I was so filled with love and forgiveness that I floated ever so gently back into her body. . . . I re-entered through the top of the head, feeling the need to shrink and then squeeze back into the tight form Phyllis's body offered.[9]

As Phyllis experienced and as expressed by Kenneth Ring:

What kills is judgment; what heals is love. The Light itself is only love, and it never judges; instead it gently nudges you toward your essential self. It wants you to realize that your core being is this Light—it is not something external to you. When you become identified with this Light, you will have only love and compassion for yourself—and for everything—and you will be able to let go of all judgment. Self-condemnation, guilt, and other forms of self-laceration likewise are vanquished. When judgment—that ruthless sower of division—falls away, there is only acceptance—of everything. And that is called love.[10]

A Life Review by Any Other Name . . .

When I (Dennis) read the above accounts of life reviews, I am reminded of an experience I had when I was eighteen. At the time, I was a very scrupulous person, all wrapped up inside myself. I had entered the Jesuit religious order a few months before, and we novices were each asked to give an account of our life to another Jesuit. I wrote out what I wanted to say on eight pages, single-spaced, filled with all the things I believed I had done wrong and hated about myself. Then I shared all this with Joe, an older Jesuit I trusted. When I finished, Joe came over and hugged me. I was totally shocked and surprised. Although my so-called "sins" were the fumblings of a confused child raised in a rigidly religious home, to me they were worthy of eternal damnation. Yet Joe's response was to hug me.

I felt Joe's hug, which I would now call an experience of non-judgmental unconditional love, in the deepest part of my being. I sobbed uncontrollably. From that moment on, I began to change from being a scrupulous person tied up within myself to being a person in love with life. I believe that in that hug I was given an important part of my identity: as a brother to all and as one who could love much because he had been forgiven much.

Since that time, many people have asked me to listen to them as Joe listened to me. For example, members of Twelve-Step groups have asked me to listen to their fifth step, which is something like a life review, and participants in our seminars have asked if they could share with me aspects of their lives about which they feel guilty or ashamed. Many of these people then changed dramatically, just as I did. For my part, non-judgmentally listening to others share their version of a life review (and usually giving them a hug at the end) has helped me experience my identity as a brother. It has also allowed me to experience what NDErs remind us is our essence: unconditional love.

Sooner Is Better Than Later

The life review comes in many forms, and most great spiritual and healing traditions have their own version. We do not have to nearly die in order to receive its benefits. As Denny experienced, we can review our life here and learn from it, rather than waiting until we die. This can help us to live better, as in Denny's case, and to die better, as in the following story.

June's father was hateful to everyone in their town and was known as "that mean old Yankee who lives on Oak Street." This made it impossible for her mother, Brit, to maintain friendships. June believed that the stress of living with her father led to Brit's death of a heart attack when June was ten. When June was thirty-eight, her father was diagnosed with pancreatic cancer and told that he would not live long. June describes what happened shortly before he died:

> I was sitting on the porch and he came out with deep concern on his face. "June," he said, "there is no way I can make it up to all of those people I've hurt over the years. But Brit came to me last night and said she was coming soon to take me away and to make amends before I leave."

June and her father agreed that they would go to the home of every person in town to whom he had been mean and abusive, and he would offer a heartfelt apology. It took three weeks for him to reach everyone. Then he was ready to die:

> On the day my father died, he was peaceful and calm. He asked for water, but other than that we sat completely transfixed by a beautiful music that seemed to be just coming out of the air. "Do you hear that music?" my father said. "I've never heard anything like that." Neither had I. He lay down on the couch and seemed to almost shut off. Then, to my surprise, it seemed as though a spirit body of him sat up. It was beaming with joy. I heard him say, "good-bye," and right in front of him stood my mother and aunt . . . my mother was looking at me with great joy. And then that was it. The spirit bodies faded away and I was alone with my father's body.[11]

This story reminds us of our friend, Bill Carr. When Bill was diagnosed with cancer and given six months to live, he made a list of fifty people with whom he needed reconciliation. He bought a van and spent those six months driving around the United States, visiting nearly every person on his list. This brought Bill so much healing that he lived for six more years rather than six months.

Healing Process

Whether we have a long time left to live, as Denny did when he reviewed his life with Joe, or a short time, as did June's father and Bill Carr, we can change our life now. How might you live differently if you knew that when you die, you will experience your effect on everyone you interacted with in your life? This will happen during the life review in an environment of infinite love. Since the purpose of the life review is our own growth in love and compassion, it would seem that the more we reflect upon our effect on others here, the more we can live in the Light and as the Light. We move in this direction every time we honestly face how we have hurt another, forgive ourselves, make amends, and use our self-awareness to grow. The following process is intended as an opportunity to do this.

In the life review during an NDE, the experiencer can stop the process at any time in order to rest in unconditional love for as long as needed. We encourage you to do the same in the process that follows. Go through only as many steps of the process as you can while maintaining a sense of your own goodness and of being held in love. If you feel yourself getting caught in self-judgment, stop and return to Steps 2 to 4. There is no hurry to complete this process; you can return to it whenever you feel ready.

1. Close your eyes and put your feet flat on the floor. Breathe slowly and deeply. Place your hand on your heart and imagine that you are breathing in and out through your heart.

2. Recall a moment from your life when you experienced unconditional, non-judgmental love, a moment when you knew your goodness. Hold those feelings in your heart and let them grow there.

3. Now imagine that you have died and are in the presence of the Light. It is far brighter than any light you have ever seen, but it does not hurt your eyes. The Light is alive and loving. The love you experience is at least a million times greater than the moment you just recalled, and your sense of your essential goodness is that much greater as well. Rest in this for as long as you wish, continuing to breathe in and out through your heart.

4. Now let your life review begin. First recall moments when you were kind and loving to others, including the natural world, such as plants, animals, or the earth. Let feelings of appreciation for yourself grow in your heart, as you continue to breathe deeply.

5. Recall a moment when someone hurt you, someone for whom you were able to feel understanding and compassion because you had some sense of the circumstances and/or wounding underlying that person's behavior. Relive letting go of judgment and holding this person in love. Once again, let feelings of appreciation for yourself grow in your heart, as you continue to breathe deeply.

6. When you are ready, recall one moment when you believe you hurt another person or some aspect of creation. Choose a moment that you feel ready and able to face. Let the scene unfold in your imagination, as you breathe in the infinite, unconditionally loving Light that enfolds you. Recall the moment you got in touch with in the previous step, when you were able to hold a person who hurt you in non-judgmental love. Continue only so long as you can maintain this same attitude of unconditional, non-judgmental love toward yourself. If you notice any feelings of shame or self-judgment, stop and go back to Steps 2 to 4.

7. What needs or hurts within yourself might have affected
    your attitudes and actions toward this person? Is there any
    way you still need to care for yourself?

8. How do you imagine your attitudes and actions might have
    affected the other person? Is there any way you want to
    reach out to that person now?

9. Repeat this process with as many memories as you wish of
    moments when you believe you hurt another person or some
    other aspect of creation.

Reflection Questions

What touched me most in this chapter is . . .

When I reflect upon this chapter in relation to my life,
I feel . . . I want . . .

⌒ 13 ⌒

Purpose: Why Am I (Still) Here?

Gordon Allen was such a successful businessman that he was
named "CEO of the Year" by *Financial World* and "Tycoon
of the Decade" by *Success!* He was featured on the covers of both
magazines. He was a ruthless financier, who described making
money as "what really made me run. . . . I *enjoyed* making money."

While hospitalized for acute pneumonia, Gordon had an
NDE. He experienced love that "was so unconditional, it was
overwhelming to me. . . . And . . . the sense of this very profound
love was followed by a sense of purposefulness, that whatever
was happening had a point to it." Then he was greeted by three
"spiritual beings" as "an old friend and a loved brother." He was
told that he could stay if he wished. However, he understood that

> *I had not finished what I was sent to do. . . . The thought was
> communicated to me that all the skills and all the talents and
> everything I'd been given . . . were for a purpose greater than the
> purpose that I had used them for. The purpose of making money
> in itself wasn't it. . . . And that they should now be applied in
> some ways that would be shown to me. Absolutely, that's the
> moment when my life changed.*

When Gordon recovered, he "decided that I was not going to try to save anything that I had from my past life in the financial world." He called the people who had been most dependent upon him as a financial guru:

And I'd say, "Hi, Bill," or "Hi, Jack," or whoever it was, "This is Gordy. You remember how . . ." And they'd say, "Oh, yeah, Gordy . . ." And you could hear them pull off the phone because they're waiting for the hit, because in the old days that might have been a hit coming after them, looking for the money or whatever I was doing. And I'd say, "You know, last time we talked I really wasn't too happy about the way that came out, and I think I would be less than candid if I didn't say I was not being good to you, that I wasn't being loving to you. And I just wanted to call you and ask your forgiveness for whatever I might have done to you."

Now, if you want to hear dead air on a telephone, do that. You'd have total silence. And then there's a little stutter, and they'd say, "Well, I guess so," or whatever, and that's the end of it.

Gordon became a counselor, helping others change their lives. Although he lives simply, Gordon says, "The richness of the life that I have today is like the Sistine Chapel compared to a plain, drab little room somewhere."[1]

We Came Here for a Reason

One of the hallmarks of a feeling of happiness and fulfillment in life is the sense that "I am doing what I came here to do," accompanied by a profound sense of rightness and purposefulness. A common experience of NDErs is returning with a deepened or clarified understanding of their purpose. In Gordon's case, his understanding of his purpose was turned inside out.

Sometimes, like Gordon, the NDEr knows that his or her life must change, but does not yet know how. Other times, the life review in an NDE includes specific guidance or at least clues as to the special purpose of one's life. For example, while delivering her first child, Maria had an NDE, in which she passed through the tunnel and into the Light. What follows is translated from her native Swedish:

There was a being in the light, neither male nor female, only a being, sending out all the unconditional love and wisdom of the universe, and I wanted to express with tears my feeling of blessedness. I was one with the light. . . ."

The being in the light told me I had to return to life, taking care of my son. "No," I said, "it's a mistake. I was supposed to get a daughter." But the entity insisted, "No, you have given life to a son!" I also got the information that I must stay calm, when returning, because "the doctors will tell you that your son is very ill due to lack of oxygen to his brain, and will most probably die. But don't worry, your son will live; he will only sleep for five months, and then wake up and grow up to be a very intelligent young man. . . ."

Waking up, I was told that I had got a son who was very ill, lying in an incubator. . . . On the third day the doctors told my husband and me that our son was very ill, and was to die, because of lack of oxygen in his brain during the childbirth. But I said: "No, he will only sleep for five months, and then wake up. He'll be well!" They all looked terrified at me, and the doctor just explained that it is common that mothers can't bear information like this, and it could take some time for me to accept. But now, I know I was right. And after a little more than five months my child one day looked at me with alert eyes. Today, four years later, he can do things normal to a five- to six-year-old child.[2]

The above experience includes the NDEr seeing future events that had to do with her purpose. Like Maria, about one-third of NDErs who can recall a life review have visions of future events in their lives, and these often have to do with their purpose in life.[3]

A second example of experiencing one's purpose during an NDE is that of Eileen, who began bleeding profusely during a miscarriage. Her husband rushed her to the emergency room, where worried doctors tried to stop the bleeding. Eileen left her body and experienced herself moving toward the Light. She saw her beloved grandmother ahead of her, and in her grandmother's arms was Eileen's miscarried baby daughter. Eileen experienced so much love, joy, and attraction to the Light and the people in it that she wanted to go completely into it. Then she heard a gentle voice saying, "Look behind you. You have a choice." As she looked back, she saw her distraught husband holding her physical hand. She loves her husband dearly and realized that part of her purpose here is to be physically connected to him. Eileen knew she could neither take him with her nor break the physical connection by leaving him. As soon as she decided she must return to her husband, she was back in her body. The bleeding stopped immediately, she sat up, and she felt entirely well. Over the doctors' objections, Eileen and her husband went home.

By definition, an NDE results in coming back to this life, as Eileen did. One only *nearly* dies, and the reason consistently given for returning is that the NDEr has not yet completed the purpose of his or her life. In Eileen's case, she had not yet finished loving her husband in this world. In Maria's case, she needed to care for her newborn son. As in these examples, sometimes NDErs return with a clear sense of their purpose. More often, it becomes evident over time. This may happen in a natural and organic way; as NDErs compare their experience of infinite and unconditional love with their human life, often what they have been doing appears increasingly meaningless.

For example, in Chapters 11 and 12, we shared the story of Barbara, whose childhood abuse was healed during her NDE. After she returned, she realized that her life before had been devoted to materialism:

I wasn't living authentically. . . . We had the perfect house and the perfect cars. We had an airplane and a swimming pool . . . but it was hollow. And after the experience . . . the materialism wasn't important any more. I went back to school, and I became a respiratory therapist, and I worked in ICU, and my patients were telling me about their experiences. This became the real, authentic me.

Barbara later became a psychotherapist, working with children and adults who had been abused, and a near-death researcher. She has also been at the bedsides of many dying people, helping them on their way.[4]

Whether the process is immediate or gradual, NDErs typically return to find a new or deeper sense of the purpose of their life. Following are typical examples that combine elements from various NDEs:

- A policeman finds that he can no longer shoot a gun or kill anyone after his NDE, and he becomes a high school teacher.

- A corporate attorney, who once cared only about winning cases, now cares more about her clients as human beings, and she seeks an environment of greater emotional authenticity. She goes off to live with and learn from indigenous people, with only the belongings she can carry in her backpack.

- A man who had been involved in organized crime leaves that world, and he becomes a counselor for delinquent students.

- A fundamentalist preacher no longer believes his own sermons about punishment and hell. He realizes that now all he can preach about is unconditional love. He has to leave his church . . . actually, he gets himself thrown out for not being "orthodox" enough.

In all these examples, because the NDEr is now aligned with his or her own real self, the path that is congruent with the real self becomes evident and whatever is incongruent has to be set aside.

Sometimes, rather than the gradual and organic discovery of one's purpose described above, the sort of obvious guidance that one receives during an NDE is given, but at a later time. For example, during his NDE David Milarch, a tree nurseryman, passed through a white light so brilliant that he described it as "like a goddamn blowtorch!"[5] He was told that for the planet's survival the DNA of old-growth trees must be kept alive.[6] He had no idea just how he was to do this. A few months later, he was awakened at 1:00 a.m. when his bedroom lit up. He said,

> It was like three or four cars were shining their lights in the window, and it scared the starch out of me. . . . I put my hands over my eyes and heard a female voice say, "Get a pad and pen and go to your leather chair and write this down." So I said, "If you turn the lights down I'll do whatever you want." They dimmed the lights and I got a pad and pen and sat in my recliner. I don't remember anything after that until six, when I got up to wake the kids for school. And there on the pad were ten pages of an outline. I'd never written an outline in my life. I hadn't written too much at all. . . . That's how this project was born.[7]

When David showed the outline to his wife, although it did look like his writing, she said, "You couldn't have written this, there aren't any spelling mistakes and you can't spell."[8]

David's project was to clone the oldest and hardiest trees in the world, those that would be most resistant to climate change, to create "a kind of Noah's ark of tree genetics."[9] Although scientists and tree experts told him it was impossible, David and his team have successfully cloned giant redwoods and sequoias in the United States, and they have been invited to other countries to clone their ancient trees as well.[10]

The Light Will Help All of Us Find Our Purpose

Most of us have not had an NDE. Yet, we come here with a purpose, and guidance in finding it is available to us all. The renowned Swiss psychiatrist Dr. Elisabeth Kubler-Ross, author of the classic book *On Death and Dying*, experienced this in a quite dramatic way. She studied near-death experiences and eventually had one herself. However, the following experience occurred prior to her own NDE. Dr. Kubler-Ross had interviewed Mrs. Schwartz, who had an NDE and then lived for another year and a half. Ten months after Mrs. Schwartz died, Dr. Kubler-Ross was thinking of discontinuing her seminar on death and dying at the University of Chicago. Following is an account of her experience with the deceased Mrs. Schwartz:

After giving her lecture on death and dying in a classroom, she was discussing shutting down the seminar with a minister who had worked with her in the program. As they approached an elevator, where the minister would leave her, Ross noticed a woman standing in front of the elevator. The woman looked familiar, but Ross could not immediately place her. As soon as the minister got on the elevator, the woman, who Ross described as being somewhat transparent, approached her and asked her if she could accompany her to her office. Dr. Ross came to realize that it was Mrs. Schwartz and began to question her own awareness.

"This was the longest walk of my life," Ross related. "I am a psychiatrist. I work with schizophrenic patients all the time, and

I love them. When they would have visual hallucinations I would tell them." She told herself that she was seeing Mrs. Schwartz but that it couldn't be. She did a reality check on herself and wondered if she had seen too many schizophrenic patients and was beginning to see things herself.

"I even touched her skin to see if it was cold or warm, or if the skin would disappear when I touched it. It was the most incredible walk I have ever taken, not knowing why I was doing what I was doing. I was both an observing psychiatrist and a patient."

When they reached Ross'[s] office door, Mrs. Schwartz opened it and told Ross that she had come back for two reasons, first to thank her and the Reverend Gaines, a former minister in the program, for the help they had given her, and, secondly, to ask her not to stop her work on death and dying.

Ross got to her desk and did another reality check, touching her desk, chair, and a pen. "I was hoping she would disappear," Ross continues the story. "But she didn't. She just stood there and lovingly said, 'Dr. Ross, did you hear me? Your work is not finished. We will help you and you will know when the time is right, but do not stop now. Promise?'"

As a further test of her awareness or sanity, Ross asked the woman if she would write a note to Reverend Gaines. Mrs. Schwartz complied. She then got up from her chair, and said, "Dr. Ross, you promise," to which Ross replied, "I promise." With that Mrs. Schwartz disappeared.

Ross kept the note and later told the story to many friends and associates. She considered having fingerprint and handwriting experts examine the note to see if they matched up with the fingerprints and handwriting of Mrs. Schwartz, but she never got around to it and eventually gave the note to the Rev. Renford Gaines. Researcher Boyce Batey later contacted Gaines, who

. . . *provided Batey with the exact wording, viz.* "Hello there, Dropped in to see Dr. Ross. One of two on the top of my 'list.' You being the other. I'll never find or know anyone to take the place of you two. I want you to know, as I've told her, I'm at peace at home now. I want you to know you helped me. The simple Thank you is not enough. But please know how much I mean it. Thank you again. Mary Schwartz."

At the time, Dr. Ross was still very much the skeptic when it came to such things. "I didn't believe in all that stuff," she expresses her attitude at the time of the encounter with Mrs. Schwartz.

Of course, Dr. Kubler-Ross did continue her work and became one of the foremost authorities in the world on death and dying. She also came to believe in a spirit world, and she wrote,

Death is simply a shedding of the physical body like the butterfly shedding its cocoon. It is a transition to a higher state of consciousness where you continue to perceive, to understand, to laugh, and to be able to grow.[11]

Do What Makes You Happy

In Dr. Kubler-Ross's case, the guidance she needed to help her follow her life purpose came through an extraordinary intervention from the other side, in the form of a visit from Mrs. Schwartz. For most of us, this guidance is far more subtle and comes from promptings of the Light from within ourselves in the direction of what will bring us the most happiness.

For example, Pat worked at the development office on the Sioux reservation, recording donations. He chain-smoked and rarely smiled; he usually appeared depressed. His wife knew he was not happy, and she urged him to go on a retreat to reflect on his life. Pat was more than willing, since he sensed that his life did not match his inner sense of himself.

During the retreat, Pat was encouraged to imagine himself on his deathbed, looking back on his life at this moment, and ask himself, "What do I wish I had done differently?" Over the next few days, as he reflected on this question, it became very clear to him that he was totally bored with his clerical work at the development office. It also became clear to him that what resonated most with his inner sense of himself was counseling alcoholics. He was deeply concerned by the 95 percent rate of alcoholism on the reservation, and he wanted to help in any way he could. He also wanted to work with his wife, who was an alcoholism counselor.

He left the retreat knowing that this was the right course for him. When he returned to the reservation, he quit his job at the development office and went to school for training in alcoholism counseling. He quit smoking. He laughed freely and often. He loved his work. The Light within Pat had gently guided him toward the purpose of his life, and his happiness was the sign that he had found it.

Pat did not have an NDE. Peggy did, and it taught her a similar lesson about the importance of doing what she loved:

> One thing I [learned] was that we are ALL here to do an "assignment of love." We don't have to do it at all, or we can do as many as we like. It's up to us . . . it is the very thing or things we love most. I was such a bozo. I always thought doing what you loved most was selfish. I can remember how amazed and happy I was when this information "came into my mind." This other source of energy, using my voice, said, "That is the most unselfish and constructive thing you can do for the world because that is your assigned energy and you will be happiest doing it, best at it, and most respected for it!"

During my NDE, I did recall what it was like for me when I was
around seven years old and singing all the time. I literally relived
those moments and felt the joy I had known when I used to sing.
I recalled the light telling me to try to go toward singing. It said
nothing of fame, money, or even a nice singing voice.[12]

Peggy's story may be somewhat startling because it includes none of the "shoulds" with which most people were raised. Her purpose is not framed first of all in terms of how she can help the world or serve humanity. Rather, the only criterion for identifying her purpose is: What does she love most? As it turns out, doing this is the best thing she can do for others as well . . . but that is not the starting point. The starting point is only what gives her joy, not what she *should* do.

Pat's and Peggy's experiences echo the words of Kenneth Ring:

Everyone is loved infinitely, and with incredible compassion.
There is a plan or, one might say, a kind of blueprint for every-
one's life, and, while we each are free to embrace or reject it, the
Light is there to help us find it. If we can open ourselves to the
Light, invoke it into our lives, we will, in time, be shown our own
way—and we will recognize it unmistakably because it will give
us joy. Joy in living is the truest sign that we are living right.[13]

Our Purpose Continues

Finding and expressing what gives us joy seems to continue in the next life. We last left Jan Price's springer spaniel Maggie on a green love seat with her paws spread across Jan's lap. (See Chapter 7.) Maggie then invited Jan to continue on a tour of the other side. They came to the Temple of Knowledge, where a group of writers was sharing ideas in a lively discussion. Other individuals were joyfully painting at their easels, playing musical instruments, dancing "with ethereal grace," caring for plants, playing sports, and so forth. Evidently an infinite number of possibilities exist for joyfully continuing to carry out our purpose.

Moreover, purpose on the other side seems to be linked to purpose here. For example, in the Temple of Knowledge, groups who were studying together were broadcasting to interested people on earth "seed ideas" on everything from ancient philosophies to new scientific discoveries and inventions. This may be one reason why people in different places on earth sometimes make the same discovery or arrive at the same new understanding at almost exactly the same time.[14]

Perhaps another way to get in touch with our purpose is to ask ourselves what we would most love doing when we cross over to the other side. Finding our purpose here may be just the beginning of enjoying it forever.

Healing Process

1. Close your eyes and put your feet flat on the floor. Breathe slowly and deeply. Place your hand on your heart and imagine that you are breathing in and out through your heart.

2. Be aware of your Light, the Light that is your essence. Experience how it fills your being and radiates out from you.

3. If you imagine yourself on the other side, where there are musicians, painters, scientists, gardeners, inventors, and children to care for, what is it that you would most like to do? Listen not for what you think you "should" do, but rather for what you truly love, for what makes you happy.

4. Are there ways you are already doing this here, or are there ways in which you can begin to do it or do more of it?

5. You might wish to return to this process over time, and watch for a gradually growing awareness of the purpose of your life.

Reflection Questions

What touched me most in this chapter is . . .

When I reflect upon this chapter in relation to my life, I feel . . . I want . . .

≈ 14 ≈

The Examen: A Daily Life Review and a Way to Find Our Purpose

The previous chapters, 10, 11, and 12, focused upon the life review. Chapter 13 focused upon finding the special purpose of our life. For many years, we have done a process every evening that is a daily version of the life review and also the best way we know (short of having it revealed to us during an NDE) of finding the purpose of our life.

The Examen

This morning, I (Sheila) was worrying about how to handle a situation involving a friend who is having a very difficult time emotionally and appears to be acting out this difficulty in his relationships with others. I have felt unsure whether to intervene or wait for him to seek help on his own. I decided to wait, because in this way I can better protect myself and my family. I said to Denny, "I'm trying to imagine myself reliving this situation during my life review after I die. I wonder if what I am doing will seem the most loving choice to me then?"

Since the three of us have begun to catch the benign virus of the NDE, we often find ourselves asking this kind of question.

We know from our studies of NDEs that nothing will be lost, and we'd rather get it right while we are still here than have to face our failures of love later. For example, while I was staying with Sheila and Denny, I (Matt) had to decide whether to go to my nephew John's lacrosse game. As the team's goalie, he has a lot of responsibility, and he appreciates all the support he can get. The game was three hours away, which meant that if I went I would be giving up a whole day and spending it out in the cold (the forecast was twenty-eight degrees Fahrenheit with a twenty mile per hour wind). If I did not go, I could get a lot of work done in my warm, cozy room. It seemed like a no-brainer. I would stay.

But, since I was trying to make decisions in light of the NDE life review, I decided to see if that would change anything. First I imagined myself watching my life review if I stayed home and then if I went. I imagined myself in John's shoes, feeling how much it meant to him to have me come and how we would get closer afterwards as we shared the game's highlights. Going to the game would be more loving than staying in my room and doing the work I could do another day. Again, it seemed like a no-brainer, but this time with the opposite outcome. I went to the game. John's team won 15–4, and I was there to celebrate with him. That is one of the moments I most look forward to reliving in my life review.

The Examen Can Guide Us

We believe a process we call "the examen" can help us live now in a way we'll be proud of later. For many years, we have used this process to reflect on each day's experience. We now realize that it is a kind of daily life review.

As we have used the examen ourselves and taught it to others as the final presentation at all our retreats, it is based on two questions:

What am I most grateful for today?

What am I least grateful for today?

Since we assume that our nature is love and that our deepest desire is to contribute to the well-being of others, we are not surprised that normally at the end of a day we are most grateful for moments when we lived as the love that we are and extended that to others. (See Chapter 10.) Conversely, our moments of least gratitude are normally those moments when we were furthest from ourselves and behaved in an unloving way toward ourselves or others.

One benefit of doing the examen on a daily basis is that we begin to see patterns over time, including aspects of ourselves that need growth and healing. Then our examen can focus on these patterns. For example, if a recurring issue in our examen is dealing with a person we find intimidating, we might ask ourselves, "When today was I able to speak to that person I'm so afraid of without compromising my self-respect?" Or, if a recurring issue is losing patience with our child, we might ask ourselves, "When today, as I kept passing by my daughter's messy room, did I feel best about how I handled my feelings?"

Thus, the examen seems to us to be something of a practice or dry-run for the life review . . . and, hopefully, a way to spare ourselves some regret later. Consider the following example of a couple who are thinking along the same lines as they look forward to being in the "movie" of their life review:

> *Learning about the life review has definitely improved my husband's demeanor! Now, whenever he begins to lose his temper, he wants me to head him off with the words, "Remember, movie time!" He is dreading the day when he will find out what it's like to be me, listening to his rantings and lectures on various topics. I remind him that both of our "movies" will include joyful scenes as well as sad ones. These days he is trying very hard to insure the second half of his movie will be applause-worthy!*[1]

The examen can be done alone, but usually we do it together. Note that in the example above, the husband is concerned about what it is like for his wife to listen to him. He knows that in his life review, he will experience this from within her. When the examen is done with another, we can participate in this aspect of the life review here and now, as well. This is true because sometimes what for one of us is the moment of most gratitude is the moment of least gratitude for another, and sharing the examen gives us a chance to enter into another's heart.

For example, our favorite country is Guatemala, and my (Denny's) favorite recreation there is bartering in artisan markets, where everything is made by hand with beautiful, rainbow colors. One evening, during a trip to Guatemala, I shared with Sheila and Matt that I was most grateful for being able to buy six hand-woven shirts. Because I had bartered the price per shirt down from $12 to $4, I had bought one for myself and five for my friends. That same evening Sheila reported my bartering as her moment of least gratitude. Sheila makes things by hand (she knitted sweaters for everyone in our family), and she knew that each shirt would take about five days to make. So when the seller said, "$12," rather than me offering $4, Sheila wanted me to say "$24."

We returned to Guatemala again two years later. This time, before I bartered in the market, I bartered with Sheila about what would be a fair price. She understood my delight in buying beautiful, handmade shirts for myself and my friends, and I understood her concern that native craftspeople be treated fairly and appreciated. At the end of that day, when we did the examen, we all agreed that our moment of most gratitude was the shirt purchase we made, in which both the seller and ourselves felt like winners. Thus, the examen had allowed us to develop the empathy and compassion that is a fundamental lesson of the life review.

We might also think of the examen as a way of reflecting each day on how fully we lived as the Light that we are and followed its guidance, which is always available to us. Many years after her NDE, one woman reflected on how her experience had changed her life:

Over time, as I engaged in spiritual practices to examine and transform the dark sides within myself, I developed an increased consciousness that a greater spirit was operating in my life, as opposed to viewing life as a series of random, meaningless events. . . . This required attunement to the existence of spirit at work in every aspect of my life, seeing people, places, and things as teachers and as channels by which the Light was trying to communicate with me, offer guidance, and teach me what I needed to learn.[2]

Healing Process

Near-death experiences suggest that when we die, every moment we lived will be part of our life review. That includes today; sometime in the future, we'll each be looking at today in the presence of the Light. In this process, we invite you to do the examen now as if you had just died.

1. Close your eyes and put your feet flat on the floor. Breathe slowly and deeply. Place your hand on your heart and imagine that you are breathing in and out through your heart.

2. Imagine yourself in the presence of the Light and doing your life review.

3. Ask yourself the following questions:

   When today did I live in a way that I would be really happy to relive after I die?

   When today did I live in a way that I would not want to relive after I die? How might I live this moment differently if I am in a similar situation again?

The Examen Helps Us Find Our Purpose

In addition to being a form of daily life review, the examen can also help us find our special purpose. As we do the examen regularly, we begin to see a pattern.

This pattern can alert us to moments which at first we might easily pass by as insignificant but that ultimately can give direction for our lives.

For example, one day we were giving an English/Spanish conference in the United States, where the Anglos played music in the morning and the Hispanics played in the afternoon. That evening when we did the examen, the moment all three of us were least grateful for was the same: the way the conference had dragged when the Anglos played. Our moment of most gratitude was also the same: the Hispanic group and how their music revived the conference.

At first glance, those two moments seemed insignificant. But during the next few months, we all noticed a pattern in which often our moments of gratitude centered around Hispanic people. If this had happened only a few times, we might have ignored it. But because we did the examen regularly, and Hispanics were so often what brought us gratitude, we realized we were in touch with something significant. We finally took time to ask ourselves what we should do about it. We knew that, whenever possible, we should do more of whatever gives us the most life or gratitude. So, we decided to study Spanish in Bolivia. During the twenty-five years since then, we have worked in Latin America every year. Our experience there and the friendships we have formed with Latin American people have enriched our lives more than we can say. Our John, who has always traveled with us, has grown up not only bilingual but bicultural as well.

Our decision to study Spanish was one of the most beneficial of our lives and has allowed each of us to carry out our purpose in ways we could never have foreseen. Our experience is that when we pay attention each day to seemingly insignificant moments, they will often form a pattern of what brings us gratitude. This pattern becomes significant, because as we do more of what leads to gratitude, we will be taking another step in carrying out the purpose of our life.

Healing Process

Following is the same process as above, but this time with a focus on the pattern of what brings you gratitude.

1. Close your eyes and put your feet flat on the floor. Breathe slowly and deeply. Place your hand on your heart and imagine that you are breathing in and out through your heart.

2. Imagine yourself in the presence of the Light and doing your life review.

3. Ask yourself the following questions:

    When today did I live in a way that I would be really happy to relive after I die?

    When today did I live in a way that I would not want to relive after I die? How might I live this moment differently if I am in a similar situation again?

4. As you do this process regularly, do you notice a pattern to what would make you happy to relive after you die, in other words, to what brings you gratitude?

5. Is there any way you can do more of this? What might this pattern be saying to you about the purpose of your life?

Reflection Questions

What touched me most in this chapter is . . .

When I reflect upon this chapter in relation to my life, I feel . . . I want . . .

~ 15 ~

Who Cares for Us from the Other Side?

In the previous two chapters, we focused on our unique purpose in life, a purpose that often becomes especially clear to NDErs, but that we all bring with us into this world. As we try to carry out the unique purpose of our life, who among us would not want an infinitely and unconditionally loving presence to watch over us, guide us on our way, and hold us close? That, according to Kenneth Ring, is exactly what we have:

> . . . in every case we have considered, the individual encounters some kind of a presence within the Light, someone or something that gives the impression of having an omniscient knowledge of the person and an infinite solicitude for his or her welfare and future well-being. When we nearly die then, we find that we are not alone and presumably have never been alone. We have someone or something that appears to guide us benevolently, albeit invisibly, in our life on this earth, but that can intervene at critical moments and, even, as in the near-death state, manifest clearly into our awareness. This in itself is profoundly reassuring.[1]

Whether or not we are aware of it, the presence within the Light is with us across the entire continuum of awareness, from the most ordinary moments of earthly human life to the furthest reaches of the most complete NDE, and at every stage in between. For example, following are two stories of physical healing through the intervention of someone from the other side. The first is by Anna, who was hospitalized for peritonitis following a hysterectomy and who needed emergency surgery.

Fifteen minutes before I was taken to the operating theater, I was lying in my hospital bed feeling overwhelmed with pain. Suddenly my awareness changed, and the room became filled with a bright light . . . beside my bed, appeared my late grandfather, clad in a white coat. (He had been a general practitioner/doctor during his life. However, I had never met him, as he had died when I was seven years old!) He spoke to me about the details of my medical issues and pointed out in terms of centimeters exactly where in my abdomen the three main internal infections were located. He specified this medical information in Latin (I don't speak Latin, but I understood him) and then he . . . disappeared. . . . I was able to repeat everything my grandfather had just told me, while the surgeon wrote down detailed notes and my husband listened.

A couple of days after the (successful) surgery, I talked with the surgeon. . . . He said that my grandfather's directions had told him to move certain internal organs aside to get to the third infected location. Without my grandfather's information, he could easily have missed it, especially since at admission, they had diagnosed me with only two internal infections, not three. It was exactly as my grandfather had described it. He had said that there was an area of infected fluid in a "hidden" part of my pelvis and had described, in terms of centimeters, exactly where to drain this infected fluid. It was beneath a bleeding point.[2]

The second story of physical healing through intervention from the other side is of Shelley Yates's son Evan. Shelley and her four-year-old son Evan were in an accident in which their car went over a guard rail and became submerged in a flooded marsh. Shelley was underwater for fifteen minutes, during which she had an NDE and met six "majestic beings." She was rescued and revived. The moment she woke up, she screamed, "Get my baby out of the lake!" By the time Evan's body was found, he had been underwater for about thirty minutes. Both Shelley and Evan were rushed to the hospital, where Evan was placed on life support. The doctors told Shelley that her child would be brain-dead and asked her permission to take him off life support.

Shelley saw an image of an empty bucket, and she heard one of the beings from her NDE say, "Fill it up." The voice explained that in order for Evan's human body to recover, his energy body needed to be filled or rebuilt. He needed a transfusion of energy, similar to a blood transfusion. Shelley was instructed to share her greatest joy with Evan so that he would have a reason to wake up and stay in this world. Shelley needed help, and she called everyone she knew. Hundreds of people came, entered Evan's room one after another, put their hands on him, and told him why they loved being here. No negativity was permitted. For three days, Evan's body continued to deteriorate. Then he woke up, looked around, and began talking to his mother. Evan recovered and Shelley maintained contact with the beings from her NDE, who have continued to guide her in transferring healing energy to the earth as she did to her son.[3]

Similar to Shelley, a benevolent being initially cared for Amy during her NDE (see Chapter 6) and then continued to watch over her after she returned:

The most significant [part of my NDE] was being close to my Guide. And when he told me it was time for my return. I have never experienced emotion that strong . . . I knew I needed to [go], but still, I was fearful, anticipating my departure and loss of this One. I cried out, "Please! I can't go without you!"

There was a pause and then he answered, "Very well."

All at once, I felt we were together. We were one. I was safe and calm. . . . Then I was back in my dark room at home. . . . I have continued to have the ability to reach, to a certain extent, my Guide. I began, right away, to meditate, and connect with my Guide.[4]

The Soul Lives Where It Loves

In the cases of Amy and Shelley, the caring beings they encountered during their NDEs were previously unknown to them. In Anita Moorjani's case, during her NDE she met her father, who had died ten years earlier. She realized that he had never really left her and had continued to care for her and her family:

It wasn't just that I understood my father—it was as though I became him. I was aware that he'd been with my entire family all through the years after he'd passed. He'd been with my mother, supporting her and watching over her; and he'd also been with me through my wedding and my illness . . . Yes, I'm here, my darling, and I've always been here—for you and our whole family!, my father communicated to me.[5]

Not only did Anita experience the abiding presence of her father, but also of her beloved best friend Soni, who had died three years previously of cancer:

It was tremendously comforting for me to reconnect with Soni's essence, for I'd missed her so much during the years since she'd gone. I felt nothing but unconditional love, both from her and for her. And then, just as I experienced that, it was as though my essence merged with Soni's and I became her. I understood that she was here, there, and everywhere. She was able to be in all places at all times for all her loved ones.[6]

The stories of Anna, Shelley, Amy, and Anita are examples of people who consciously experienced a presence caring for them in surprising ways, a presence of which they had been unaware. The same is true for all the rest of us. How many accidents are prevented by the intervention of a loved one who has passed on, as Kaaran experienced (see Chapter 6)? How many Twelve-Step meetings include all the group members on the other side? We remember the story of George H., told to us by a long-time A.A. member. Whenever George needed help, he would call on one of his Twelve-Step mentors who had passed on, and ask, "Joe B., what would you do? Steve T., what would you do?" George needed his A.A. family, and death could not keep them from being there for him.

Like George, we all long for a loving family, but not all of us have had that here in this life, or at least our experience of family love has been wounded. This was the experience of Eben Alexander (see Chapter 6), who suffered deeply from having been separated from his birth family as a baby. He describes the healing he experienced during his NDE:

Ultimately, none of us are orphans. We are all in the position I was, in that we have other family: beings who are watching and looking out for us—beings we have momentarily forgotten, but who, if we open ourselves to their presence, are waiting to help us navigate our time here on earth.[7]

I (Sheila) needed the *other family* that Eben Alexander speaks of, and the greatest gift for me of catching the NDE benign virus is a deepening of an intuition I have always had that somewhere, in another dimly remembered realm, I have the family I lacked here. My parents were both quite ill and unable to care for their children. Even more important, I think, is that the tenor or style of the extended family with which I grew up, with a couple of exceptions, was emotionally disconnected and lacking in warmth or empathy. I've sometimes joked that we couldn't have a family reunion because no one would come!

Yet, I feel something around me that holds me and knows the way. How else could I have gotten through college and graduate school with no support and no money, formed nourishing lifelong friendships, established a healthy and deeply attached family of my own, and written many books? How could I, since earliest childhood, have had such an acute understanding of the loving connection of all things, when I received so little of that in the family I came from? I think much of it must have come from *other family*, and I sense many beings around me, whose names I have forgotten for now, but who have watched over me the whole time. I know the feeling or energetic quality of these beings, and I believe I will recognize them immediately when I die. Since I have immersed myself in studying NDEs, this intuitive knowing of those who watch over me has become more real, as if it is gradually moving from very peripheral to nearly conscious awareness.

Led by Love

Unlike Sheila, I (Matt) come from a very close family, and I deeply missed my father when he died of a sudden heart attack. I especially missed him when I took over the care of my mother, who was suffering from Alzheimer's disease. When it was time to file my father's income taxes, my mother could not do it, and I was the one responsible. I found all the necessary papers except for those detailing the tax-deductible donations my father had made to charity. He had been generously giving away most of his income. I knew he would want to get a tax deduction, so his estate could care for my mother and also continue to give to charity.

I searched for the missing papers and found nothing. Finally, I sat in my dad's chair and breathed in and out unconditional, infinite love until I felt one with that love in my dad. Then I said, "Dad, I am going to start searching wherever your love leads me. You know where those papers are." In my imagination, I focused on the rooms in our home. I felt the most love when I got to my parents' bedroom closet, which I had already searched. So I asked, "Where in the closet?" I felt the most love when I visualized my father's shoes on the floor. So I went to the closet and took out all his shoes. Under the shoes was an envelope with the records of his donations.

Whether our very life is at stake, as in Sheila's case, or we need help with a practical problem in daily life, as in Matt's case, what we really need is assurance that we are not alone. The human companions we can see are not the only ones watching over us; we have many more companions whom we cannot see.

Healing Process #1

Following is the first of two healing processes to help us experience the ongoing and eternal connection that we have with those who are watching over us from the other side. This one is intended to help us clarify how we would like them to care for us.

1. Close your eyes and put your feet flat on the floor. Breathe slowly and deeply. Place your hand on your heart and imagine that you are breathing in and out through your heart. With each breath, let your awareness grow that you are love.

2. Who might be the person or persons on the other side who especially watch over you and care for you?

3. Is there some special way you would like them to care for you? Imagine them very near to you, watching over you and caring for you in these ways. Breathe deeply, taking in their

care for you. Notice any images, sensations, or intuitions that come to you, especially surprises.

4. Is there a special way they want to care for others through you, as Shelley cared for her son and Matt cared for his mother? Be aware of them helping you to care for these people, or perhaps for some other aspect of life. Notice any "shoulds" that arise within you and gently set them aside. Follow only feelings of love and joy.

Are We Bothering Those on the Other Side?

Sometimes people have asked us, "Don't those who have died want to go on without worrying about us? Aren't we holding them back when we ask them to be present to us or to help us?" We might have wondered this ourselves, were it not for all the accounts we have now heard and read of the lengths to which those on the other side will go to contact us and to help us.

For example, there are numerous accounts of after-death contacts (ADCs) involving telephones, telephone answering machines, computers, pagers, radios, televisions, and so forth. An example is the story of Hilda, whose eighty-two-year-old father had died two weeks previously:

> We didn't have telephone service for two days because they were widening a two-lane street into a four-lane highway behind our house. We had a crew of telephone people in our backyard, and all the wires were disconnected and lying on the ground.

Hilda and her daughter were at home, when the telephone rang three different times. The first and second time, all they could hear was "a sound like the ocean." The third time, when Greta picked up the phone,

At first I heard the same sound, like ocean waves, but then I could hear a voice coming closer and closer.

I heard my father saying, "Hilda, Hilda, I love you." He only spoke Polish, and he told me how much he loved me.

I kept calling, "Daddy! Daddy! Daddy! I love you too!" But as soon as he spoke, his voice began fading away and was gone. . . . I looked at Greta and she asked me, "Mother, what's wrong? You look as white as a sheet!" I said, "I just heard Grandpa talking to me!"

I ran outside and spoke to the engineer in charge of the phone crew and asked him, "Are we having telephone service again?" He said, "No, ma'am. The wires are still lying here, and you won't have any service until tomorrow."

I said, "Are you sure? I just received a telephone call. Is it possible that they may have done something from the main office?" He said, "No, ma'am. There's no possibility of that whatsoever." He looked at me kind of strangely, and I felt I had better go back in the house before he thought I was crazy."[8]

Given the frequency of stories like this one, it seems that those on the other side can and want to take the initiative to contact us.

Knowing That Love Never Ends Can Heal Grief

It appears that those on the other side especially want to contact us to help heal our grief. For example, following is a story reported in the *Guardian*, one of the United Kingdom's leading newspapers:

When he felt the noose around his neck, Balal must have thought he was about to take his last breath. Seven years ago Balal, who is in his 20s, stabbed 18-year-old Abdollah Hosseinzadeh during a street brawl in the small town of Royan, in the northern province of Mazandaran [Iran]. But what happened next marked a rarity in public executions in Iran. . . . The victim's mother approached . . . and then decided to forgive her son's killer. The victim's father removed the noose and Balal's life was spared. Balal's mother hugged the grieving mother of the man her son had killed. The two women sobbed in each other's arms—one because she had lost her son, the other because hers had been saved. [The slain boy's father, Abdolghani] Hosseinzadeh said a dream prompted the change of heart. "Three days ago my wife saw my elder son in a dream telling her that they are in a good place, and for her not to retaliate. . . . This calmed my wife. . . .⁹

The story above is one of violence that could have led to even more violence were it not for the intervention of someone from the other side who helped two mothers grieve together. The following story is one of the tenderness and gentle care of a nine-year old boy who had died of leukemia and who found a creative way to comfort his grieving mother, Adele:

My son, Jeremy, died the day after Mother's Day. Three weeks later, just before I woke up, I heard him ask, "What are you going to do with my money?" I said, "What money?" And he said, "All the money that you saved for me." I had totally forgotten about Jeremy's savings account, and I didn't even know where he had hidden his savings book. I asked what he wanted me to do with it because obviously it must have been very important to him. Jeremy said, "I want you to go see Malcolm." Malcolm is a friend of mine who is a diamond wholesaler. I said, "Well, whatever is in that account isn't enough to go see Malcolm!" And Jeremy replied, "Yes it is! Just go see Malcolm, and you'll understand what I'm talking about. When you see it, you will know. You will think of me." Then he was gone and I woke up.

Although I thought this was kind of crazy, I looked around the house for my son's savings book but couldn't find it. Several days later, I happened to be in the same building as Malcolm's wholesale jewelry store. So I popped in there and started looking around. I saw a beautiful butterfly necklace with a diamond in it. It suddenly clicked what Jeremy had said. "You'll know it when you see it. It will remind you of me." My heart started pounding and I got kind of nervous. I asked Malcolm how much the necklace would cost. After some figuring and some bantering back and forth, he told me $200. I told him I would come back later.

My heart was still pounding when I went back to my office and called the bank. I explained that I couldn't find my son's savings book and wanted to know how much money was in his account. In a few minutes, I was told the amount was $200.47! I went back to Malcolm's store after work and bought the butterfly necklace with Jeremy's money. Now I don't go anywhere without it. I can touch it and say, "My son gave me this for my last Mother's Day with him!"[10]

Sudden Deaths

Sudden deaths in accidents, in which one person survives and one or more others die, can be some of the most difficult to heal, and it is often the intervention of the one(s) who have died that can help us most. For example, we met Tere during a recent trip to Mexico. When Tere was thirteen, she and seven of her friends went on a mission trip to the state of Tabasco with a nun from their school. On the way back, they were traveling on an overnight bus. At 2:00 a.m., Tere was asleep. One of her friends woke her up and asked if Tere would move so that she (the friend) and another of the girls could sit in Tere's seat and the one next to it because they wanted to talk. At first, Tere was annoyed at having been woken up. But then she thought, "I went to Tabasco to be kind and loving to the poor people there.

I should be kind to my friends also." So, she gave up her seat to the two girls and moved to another one.

Half an hour later, the bus went over a cliff. Most of the thirty-two people on the bus were killed, including three of Tere's friends and the nun. One of the girls died in Tere's arms, although Tere forgot that for a while. Tere's arms and clavicles were broken, and she had an NDE. She was taken to the hospital to recover. Her family waited to tell her about her friends because they did not want to upset her until she was better.

After several days, they began to say that they had sad news about three of the other girls. Tere stopped them and said, "I already know. They came to tell me goodbye, and I saw them going. They wanted me to know that they are well and happy." Rather than being crushed by trauma and grief, Tere was entirely at peace with the loss of her friends. Since her NDE, she has had a deep stillness that draws to her people who need someone with an open and listening heart in whom they can confide. Tere believes that something happened to her during her NDE that helps people to feel safe with her. We could feel it ourselves when we were near her.

Tere lost her friends. Traumatic as it was, for most people the loss of friends would not compare with the grief of the loss of a child. Yet, even this can be healed by an NDE. For example, several years ago Jay was driving in a rainstorm with his nine-teen-year-old daughter Carrie. He lost control of the car and it slammed into a cement pole. He recalls leaving his body, looking down at the accident, and feeling a deep peace. He heard Carrie say, "Daddy, let's walk to the light." They walked through a field filled with elm and oak trees, yellow butterflies, singing birds, and a delightful perfume scent.

Then they came to an open gate. Carrie walked through it to the other side, to be with a tall, strong person who was filled with light and very loving. There were others there also welcoming her. Jay was about to step through the gate himself, when it shut. A loving voice said that it was not his time and he was to go back. One of those with Carrie waved a "Texas wave" (side to side), just as Jay's grandfather from Texas had waved. Reluctantly, Jay returned to his body. At Carrie's funeral, Jay missed her, but he also felt a deep joy in having experienced for himself the peace of where she now was. The rest of his family could not understand how he could be so happy when he had just lost his daughter.[11]

They Are Watching Over Us

Our greatest teaching of how much those on the other side want to be with us and watch over us has been Zeke. Since he left this life, many people in our community have shared stories of contact with him. I (Denny) experienced this myself. We live high in the Rocky Mountains, and I was driving home from Denver on a dark, stormy night. In my rearview mirror, I noticed the flashing lights of a police car insisting that I pull over. I wondered to myself why any policeman would want to get out of his car on this blustery night. I was annoyed because I knew I wasn't speeding; I was actually going under the speed limit because I could barely see in all the rain.

As I pulled over to the side of the road, everything went dark. It was then I realized that because of the glare from the headlights of all the cars coming toward me from the opposite direction, I had not been aware that I had not turned on my headlights. When the police officer came, he said, "The lights on the back of your car are not working." I said, "It's worse than that! I just now noticed that I didn't even have my front lights on." The policeman asked for my driver's license. I would never drive without it, and I was sure I had it. I searched and searched, but I could not find it. By then, the thoroughly drenched policeman asked for the car registration papers so that he could verify my name. I gave him the papers, but I was dismayed to see that my name was not on them because the registration is in the name of our non-profit organization.

So, here I was driving on a mountain road in a rainstorm, without front lights or back lights and without my driver's license or any other way to identify myself. The policeman took the registration papers and went back to his car. Meanwhile, I was imagining spending the night in jail. Finally, he came back to my car window and said, "You're good to go." I said, "Do you mean to tell me that I've been driving without my lights on and without my driver's license, and you're telling me I'm good to go?" He repeated, "You're good to go."

By now the rain had let up, and I could get my first clear look at him. It was only then I realized that he had Zeke's face. He was the youngest police officer I had ever seen; he looked barely seventeen or eighteen years old. In fact, it was Zeke! But what was he doing in a police uniform? I was so shocked that I blurted out, "What's your name?" I expected him to say, "Zeke." He gave me another name, but I believe it was Zeke and that he had come to help me avoid a serious accident by making sure I turned on my lights.

We have heard many similar stories of how Zeke seems to be present to those who knew and loved him and who grieve his loss. Following is an account by Zeke's sister, Mia, that she asked us to share at his memorial service, of how her brother has become a loving and ever-present companion she cannot see.

· ·

Mia's Dream

When my parents first saw Zeke in the emergency room, they knew his spirit had already left his body. We all still tried to have hope and kept praying for him to recover. But then, the CAT scan indicated that Zeke's higher brain had died. Still, after he was moved to the pediatric ICU, I kept vigil for him. Many hours later, my mother asked me to sleep.

I left the ICU with fire in my heart and then sorrow like a
bag of stones sank to the pit of my stomach. I walked the
hospital hallways until dawn and tried to understand how we
had arrived at this lot. Finally at the Valley of my Sorrow, I
fell asleep in the hospital's family room. I slept with conflict
and anguish, the depth of which I had never known before.
I pleaded and tried to reason with a Higher Creator for an
alternative to the current outcome.

I must have drifted into delirium, and then I was soothed
with a sense of calm. I started to dream of Zeke. First, I
remember hearing his voice. He said my name, "Mia." I
listened and followed the voice, and my dream carried me
to the stairwell in our house that descends to his bedroom.
He stood two steps from the landing and looked up at me as
I stood a few steps above him. He smiled his assured Zeke
smile and said, "Mia, I'm still here. Actually, I'm downstairs." He laughed and said, "It's not a big deal." It was his
laughter that immediately calmed me down.

I followed him into his bedroom, where he stood looking
out the window at the field. He continued speaking. He said,
"Please don't worry yourself like this. You can always find
me here." Quickly our bodies transferred one floor above
his bedroom, where he looked out at the field again. He was
holding a cup of Horchata tea, wearing his grey school sweat
pants, a white long-sleeved shirt, and his father's slippers.

"I'm waiting here," he said sweetly. He repeated again, "I'm
waiting for YOU here," and he smiled at me. I knew he
meant me specifically, but I knew he meant everyone else,
specifically and yet all at once, as well.

At that moment, I awoke with a profound sense of peace
and a sense that, while I may not be able to see him and
speak with him in his physical presence, I will be able to

converse with him in a different plane. I am not alone in sensing Zeke's presence. My brother, Max, had three dreams in which Zeke seemed to be guiding us in important decisions that needed to be made with the hospital staff. After we got home, my mom's oven, which hadn't worked in three months, suddenly started working again. Zeke had promised to fix it, and we are convinced that he did.

I hope for more dreams, but even while I'm awake Zeke comes at moments when I least expect him—like the other day when my family and I were painting the deck and I knew he was right there beside me, smiling at me and saying, "Thanks for helping Mom." And I continue to experience Zeke waiting for me in nature and in other people. Zeke is alive and waiting for us; we simply cannot see him anymore.

Unfinished Business and Deepening Our Connection

As in the stories of Tere, Jay, and Zeke, knowing that our loved ones are well and that love never ends can help heal grief. The stories above are of people who seem to have a clear sense of connection to the one(s) on the other side. Love flows most freely when there is no unfinished business between us and the one for whom we grieve. What if our connection is not so clear? Sometimes one of the most painful aspects of grief can be our perception that we have unfinished business with the person who has died and our fear that it is now too late to complete it. Is it really too late? Or, what if we already do feel a strong sense of connection but we want to deepen it?

Following is a process that may help us. We have led tens of thousands of people in this process all over the world. The results have taught us that our loved ones are "alive and waiting for us" on the other side, and it is never too late.

Healing Process #2

1. Close your eyes and put your feet flat on the floor. Breathe slowly and deeply. Place your hand on your heart and imagine that you are breathing in and out through your heart. With each breath, let your awareness grow that you are love.

2. Think of someone with whom you share a bond of love who has died, and with whom you want a deeper connection. Perhaps, before this person died, you did not have a chance to share with him or her everything that was in your heart. Perhaps you had unfinished business in some other way, and you wish you had resolved that sooner. With what person who is on the other side do you want to deepen your bond of love? Who on the other side wants to deepen his or her bond of love with you?

3. Imagine this person standing before you. Is there anyone else you would like to have there with you to help the two of you connect more deeply? As you look into his or her eyes, what is in your heart that you most want to say? Breathe this out from your heart into this person's heart.

4. Look into the heart of this person, and listen to what he or she most wants to say to you. Breathe this into your heart.

5. Continue to say and do whatever will most fill both of you with life. Perhaps you wish to take this person to a favorite spot, or introduce new members of your family, or have this person fill in some hurt place in your life. If you are praying for a miscarried, aborted, or stillborn baby, perhaps you wish to name the child and welcome him or her with whatever ritual is most meaningful for you.

6. If it seems right, make a space for this person in your heart. Perhaps imagine putting a rocking chair or a candle there,

and invite him or her to make a home in your heart. As they do so, feel the warmth of his or her light filling your heart. Take deep breaths, breathing in all that this person wants to give you.

Reflection Questions

What touched me most in this chapter is . . .

When I reflect upon this chapter in relation to my life, I feel . . . I want . . .

⤝ 16 ⤞

Love Heals the Body

Jonathan had esophageal surgery and was given only a 1 percent chance of survival. He describes those who lovingly cared for him in his NDE as people who looked like angels:

> [I] remember standing about ten feet up and ten feet to the side of my body on the [operating] table. . . . Around the table were at least a dozen nurses and doctors. But what was so emotional was the presence of [glowing] people that I can only describe as angels. Each angel was guiding the hands of the staff they were standing next to. I heard no noise, no voices, no music. It was peacefully quiet. I don't remember details too specific, such as what tools were used or the exact position of my body, but only because I was focused so much on the angels guiding the staff and everything they did, from walking to the use of the tools within my chest cavity. Even after the operation, I still had an unusual peace and no fear. The doctor said it was the best operation he had ever gone through—there were no problems at all—and he was impressed at my rate of recovery.[1]

Like Jonathan, people who have near-death experiences are, by definition, physically healed. They don't stay dead. Moreover, they often not only survive a life-threatening situation but also may feel truly well and whole afterwards. For example, following is the story of a diabetic Mexican woman:

Prior to her experience, she had lost the ability to see. Diabetes had taken away her retina, and her heart wasn't supplying enough circulation to her brain to allow her to speak. She was in very poor shape. They prepared her for surgery. Open-heart surgery on a diabetic woman of sixty-seven is full of risk. The doctors went outside to discuss their strategy. While they were conferring, she saw the wall open up and a brilliant light poured out. A bearded man in white stepped up beside her. He was made of white light. "You're not ready to follow me yet . . . you're not prepared. I'm going to give you back your eyesight. You'll need it to finish your life. And I'm going to heal the heart valve, so you can speak again. You still have a few more things to do. Your grandchildren need you to teach them." According to the woman's account, he placed his hand on her chest, and her eyesight returned. [Later] she sat in a wheel chair, full of confidence, and smiling . . . her eyes were clear, and she was happy in a calm way.[2]

Another example is an NDEr who was born with cerebral palsy:

As a result, he had a contracted and deformed hand, which throughout his life he had not been able to open completely. After his NDE he was able to open and use his hand for the first time in his life. This medically inexplicable healing was corroborated by his family and health-care team.[3]

Physical healing may also happen in a near-NDE, in which people who are not in any danger of death have an NDE-like experience. Dr. Elisabeth Kubler-Ross, herself an NDE researcher, describes how this happened to her:

I will never forget when I had my own personal experience after a busy and exhausting workshop. I was lifted out into a realm of such love and care, floating and uplifted as by invisible, tender arms and experienced a rejuvenation and a recharging of my energies as if half a dozen mechanics had lovingly fixed up an old car and made it new. When I returned to my physical body I felt refreshed and strong again, and I had a conviction that we are truly looked after beyond all our comprehension.[4]

We might summarize these experiences by saying that love heals the body, something we know intuitively. As Dr. Bernie Siegel writes,

I am convinced that unconditional love is the most powerful known stimulant of the immune system. If I told patients to raise their blood levels of immune globulins or killer T cells, no one would know how. But if I can teach them to love themselves and others fully, the same changes happen automatically. The truth is: love heals.[5]

The profound love of an NDE or near-NDE heals profoundly, even bringing the body back from death. This is what we would expect when we recall the essential message of the NDE, which is that we are made of light and love. We might say that illness is some way in which the cells forget who they are and how they were designed to function. Healing is remembering.

Two dramatic stories of this are those of Mellen-Thomas Benedict and Anita Moorjani, both of whom had terminal cancer. Both have described their cancer as an expression of a lack of love, in Anita's case a lack of love for herself and in Mellen-Thomas's case a lack of love for others. They each experienced themselves as healed when they discovered, during their NDEs, that they are Light and love.

Anita describes this as follows in her book *Dying to Be Me*:

> I believe that my cancer was related to my self-identity, and it feels as though it was my body's way of telling me that my soul was grieving for the loss of its own worth—of its identity. If I'd known the truth of who I actually am, I wouldn't have gotten cancer![6]

> I don't recall ever being encouraged to cherish myself—in fact, it would never even have occurred to me to do so. It's commonly thought of as being selfish. But my NDE allowed me to realize that this was the key to my healing.[7]

> Realizing that I am love was the most important lesson I learned, allowing me to release all fear, and that's the key that saved my life.[8]

> The ability to see my own magnificence and to realize that the universe and I are one and the same caused my healing.[9]

In other words, Anita's cancer was her own magnificence denied and turned inward against herself. When she owned and befriended her magnificence and let it shine outward, she was healed.

Mellen-Thomas's cancer took the form of a brain tumor. He says, "I perceived all humans as cancer, and that is what I got. That is what killed me." He was dead for an hour and a half. During this time,

I saw . . . how beautiful we all are in our essence, our core. We are the most beautiful creations. The human soul, the human matrix that we all make together is absolutely fantastic, elegant, exotic, everything. I just cannot say enough about how it changed my opinion of human beings in that instant.[10]

Mellen-Thomas recovered:

Within three days, I was feeling normal again, clearer, yet different than I had ever felt in my life. . . . I could see nothing wrong with any human being I had ever seen. . . . I remember the doctor at the clinic looking at the before and after scans, saying, "Well, there is nothing here now."[11]

Living in the Light

The healing that takes place during an NDE seems to be the result of the body remembering its innate wholeness. This remembering can be the result of various aspects of an NDE, including an in-pouring of healing love (as in the cases of the Mexican woman and Elisabeth Kubler-Ross), the recovery of love for the self (as in Anita Moorjani's case), and the recovery of love for others (as in Mellen-Thomas Benedict's case). Yet, not everyone who has an NDE is physically healed, at least not completely. The reasons for this are mysterious, as we will discuss at the end of this chapter.

However complete their physical healing, when NDErs return, they tend to gravitate toward whatever is most consistent with physical wholeness, and they usually treat their bodies with greater love and care. For example, they are attracted to alternative medicine, perhaps because it tries to help the body remember its innate wisdom and balance by working with the body's energy systems, rather than by manipulating the body with drugs.[12] Perhaps this shift is a reflection of a change in the energetic frequency of the NDEr, who has returned from an immersion in the highest frequencies of the universe.* The person will then be drawn toward what matches that higher frequency. Alternative medicine may be a better match because it emphasizes energetic (or frequency-based) methods of healing. British scientist C. W. F. McClare found that energy signals are about one hundred times more effective in conveying information to cells than are chemical signals.[13] Thus, when NDErs try to avoid chemicals in the form of pharmaceuticals, perhaps they are simply seeking out what best matches them and avoiding what does not.

Similarly, non-organic food has usually been treated with chemicals that are alien to and unrecognizable by the body. These chemicals degrade the food's natural energy, whereas whole organic foods retain more of the energy of life. Since we are made of energy in the form of light, our bodies know the difference.** NDErs may be more consciously aware of and

---

* This change expresses itself in a variety of ways, including electrical sensitivity and interference with electronic equipment in the NDEr's proximity. In their research, both P. M. H. Atwater and Kenneth Ring have found that more than 70 percent of NDErs report significant electrical sensitivity, sometimes occurring immediately after their NDE. (Kenneth Ring, Personal correspondence, September 9, 2013.) As Kenneth Ring describes it, ". . . NDErs begin to have many 'strange encounters of the electrical kind.' A surprisingly large proportion of these persons discover, for instance, that digital wrist watches will no longer work properly for them, or they 'short out' electrical systems in their cars, or computers and appliances malfunction for no apparent reason, and so on." See P. M. H. Atwater, *Coming Back to Life* (New York: Dodd, Mead & Co., 1988), 132; Kenneth Ring, *Lessons from the Light* (Needham, MA: Moment Point Press, 2006), 129.

** Kinesiological testing (sometimes known as "muscle testing") can be used to determine any substance's energetic effect on the body. For example, normally an organic apple will cause an immediate strengthening of the muscles, and an inorganic one will cause an immediate weakening. During our seminars, as we encourage participants to remember who they are, we often include a demonstration of kinesiological testing. Participants can test each other and easily see the difference in the effect on their bodies of not only organic apples versus inorganic apples, but also pure water versus soda drinks containing chemicals and sugar and/or artificial sweeteners, fresh vegetables versus processed snacks, etc. We want our participants to experience that we all have the ability to recognize what matches our Light and what does not. This ability may be undermined and muscle testing may be distorted if we consume substances that are toxic and/or to which we are allergic or sensitive. The result can be a "psychological reversal," in which our body becomes confused about what is good for it and what is not. See Blaich, *Your Inner Pharmacy*, 50–52, 150–163.

sensitive to the energy in substances such as food, since they are likely more aware of the energy in the form of light that constitutes themselves and all things. Thus, NDErs may change their diet. They may also make other changes, such as giving up smoking or drinking, exercising more, and living as close to the earth as possible.

All of us, NDErs or not, have the ability to recognize and attune ourselves to what is truly healthful and life-giving for our bodies. The more we do so, the more we are aligning our energy with the Light and the more we open ourselves to physical healing and to catching the benign virus. Conversely, the more we catch the benign virus, the more likely that we will love and care for our bodies.

Healing Process

Following is a healing process for oneself and a process for praying for healing for another. Both processes are based upon reminding our body that we are love. The latter process is one that we often use at the conclusion of our seminars. At the end of the process, we ask the group what happened. Nearly 100 percent report feeling more joy and peace. This is no small feat, given the prevalence of depression and anxiety in our culture. Of those who need some kind of physical healing, about three-fourths report some kind of immediately verifiable physical improvement, such as decreased pain or greater mobility. In some cases, at the time or later, participants report complete healing of serious conditions, such as paralysis, cancer, blindness, or deafness.

For example, we recall a seminar we gave to seven thousand villagers in the mountains of Guatemala. At the end of the healing prayer process, a shy, ancient-looking man named Joaquin stood up in front of all the people and said in his native Quiche:

For years I could not hear. When you asked us to pray in twos, my wife placed her hands on my ears and began praying. I heard a bell. Then something like a door blew open in each ear. Now I can hear everything clearly.

Why isn't everyone physically healed during this prayer, as Joaquin was, and why isn't everyone physically healed following an NDE? We can only guess. Maybe one reason is the toxic nature of much of our environment, in which our air, water, and food have been polluted; perhaps some of us are more sensitive to this than others. Perhaps we feel in our own bodies the stress and suffering of billions of other creatures, human and nonhuman, caused by war, poverty, and injustice. As Diarmuid O'Murchu puts it, "I am at all times the sum of my relationships and that's what constitutes my identity."[14] We are all in it together, and perhaps all we can ever do is remember who we are and hope that in some small way this will remind everything and everyone around us who they are.

Healing Process for Oneself

1. Close your eyes and put your feet flat on the floor. Breathe slowly and deeply. Place your hand on your heart and imagine that you are breathing in and out through your heart. With each breath, let your awareness grow that you are love.

2. See yourself as you will be after you die, perfectly and radiantly physically whole.

3. Ask yourself: What keeps me from feeling really good in this life, as I am physically here and now?

4. Whatever comes, listen lovingly to it, as you would listen to a sick child telling you where it hurts.

5. Ask your symptom: What are you trying to tell me? What do you need? What are you telling me about what separates me from the perfect physical wholeness that I am?

6. Listen carefully and consider what you can do to give your symptom what it needs so that your body can be well.

7. Once again see yourself as you will be after you die, perfectly and radiantly physically whole.

Healing Process for Another

Knowing we are made of love and light heals. When we are in touch with that for ourselves, we can help others to remember it for themselves. For us, this is the meaning of praying with another for physical healing. Positive intentions, love, and compassion are energetic signals, and when we pray for healing, those positive energetic signals directly affect the cells of the one we pray for. Reflecting on his NDE and recovery from cancer, Mellen-Thomas Benedict says:

> If something ever happened to me again, I would give faith healers and healers the first chance; I would give a miracle the first chance. If someone was all wired up and everything, I would bring a whole bunch of healers in the room . . . and let them have a go at it. I traveled the world studying these things and I've seen people healed of the most amazing things by holy water, holy places, holy men, holy women, and holy moly. I would give a miracle the first chance . . . the universe is one giant miracle and you are a part of that![15]

Physician Dr. Larry Dossey was co-chairperson of a National Institutes of Health panel that collected over 250 empirical studies of the medical effects of prayer. He concluded that "not to employ prayer with my patients was the equivalent of deliberately withholding a potent drug or surgical procedure," and "will one day constitute medical malpractice."[16] His understanding of prayer is as broad and inclusive as Mellen-Thomas's; Dr. Dossey writes:

As long as love, empathy and compassion are present, the prayer seems to work. . . . I feel there is a great lesson in tolerance in these experiments in prayer. When it comes to prayer, no religion has a monopoly.[17]

Because we are all a part of the "giant miracle" of the universe, we can be channels of healing for others when we pray for them. The healing Light that we extend when we do so is very real. For example, our friend, Carole, told us that during her NDE she could see the prayers of her loved ones for her recovery—they appeared to her as "blue lights," and with each prayer she saw one of these blue lights coming toward her. P. M. H. Atwater writes:

During my research with child experiencers of near-death states, I was continually surprised by the number of kids who saw the actual prayers being said for them, while they were out of their bodies witnessing what their loved ones were doing. They described how the power of those prayers turned into beams of radiant golden or rainbow light. . . . They showed me with gestures how that beam of light arced over from the one saying the prayer, no matter how many miles away, to where they themselves were hovering. . . .

Once a prayer beam reached them, some said it felt like a splash of love. Others said it felt warm and tickly. Because they saw prayer as real energy that did real things and had a real effect, these youngsters went on to pray easily and often.[18]

If you wish to pray with another person for healing, we suggest the following steps. This process is intended for two people, or for a larger group of people divided into twos. If you are alone and wish to pray for someone at a distance, you can adapt the following steps accordingly.

1. Close your eyes and put your feet flat on the floor. Breathe slowly and deeply. Place your hand on your heart and imagine that you are breathing in and out through your heart. With each breath, let your awareness grow that you are Light and love.

2. Recall a time when you experienced physical healing, when your cells remembered who they are. Perhaps you recovered from an illness, perhaps you were exhausted and then slept deeply, perhaps you exercised in a way that left you feeling fully alive in your body, and so forth. Let your body remember what that was like.

3. Ask yourself, What keeps me from feeling physically well and fully alive at this moment? How do I want to receive physical healing now?

4. Share with your partner how each of you would like to receive physical healing.

5. Decide who will give the prayer first and who will receive it.

6. If you are the one who is giving the prayer first, place your hand gently on the area of your partner's body that needs healing. If you prefer, you might simply take your partner's hand or put your arm around him or her.

7. Get in touch with your essence as Light and love. Imagine your Light centered in your heart and then flowing out through your arm, your hand, and into your partner. Breathe the Light out especially into whatever area of your partner's body most needs healing.

8. If you are the one who is receiving the prayer first, imagine healing Light flowing into you from your partner's hand and into your body. Breathe the Light into whatever part of your body most needs healing. See yourself perfectly and radiantly physically whole.

9. Continue to breathe deeply as you give and receive healing Light.

10. After a few minutes and when you feel ready, reverse roles so that the one who was giving the prayer now receives it and the one who was receiving it now gives it.

11. When you are ready, come back and open your eyes. Notice any changes in your body and share them with each other.

12. You may wish to repeat this process as your body continues to receive healing Light and your cells remember who they are.

Reflection Questions

What touched me most in this chapter is . . .

When I reflect upon this chapter in relation to my life, I feel . . . I want . . .

Opening Ourselves to the Benign Virus

The thesis of this book is that simply immersing ourselves in NDEs, by listening to accounts of them, reading about them, and so forth, can bring about some of the same changes in ourselves as those described in NDErs in the previous chapters. This has been our experience.

We also notice that, like NDErs and those who research them, some aspects of the NDE affect or impress each person more profoundly than other aspects. For example, Kenneth Ring emphasizes the life review in his writing, and he tells us that this is the aspect of the NDE that has been most meaningful to him. For other writers in this field, for example Anita Moorjani and Eben Alexander, the life review is not nearly so significant, and they don't even mention the life review in their books. Similarly, each of the three of us is most moved by a particular aspect of the NDE.

The Veil Is Thinner Than I Thought

For me (Matt), our ongoing connection with those on the other side has been especially moving. This idea is not entirely new to me. As children, we were taught that we could pray for those who have gone on to the next life, and they could pray for us. However, they really were gone to another world and no longer present with us in this one. The two worlds were quite distinct; those in "heaven" were up there somewhere, and we were down here. Communication between the worlds was limited and rather like sending a message to a distant outpost the old-fashioned way, by pony express rather than by email.

Immersing myself in stories of NDEs has taught me that there is no separation between me and those I love who are on the other side. They want to continue loving me even more than when they were here, with the unconditional and infinite love that they now experience. They want to share the ordinary moments of life with me, rather than being available only when I cry out for help in a crisis.

The Light is what makes the difference. As I open myself to the stories of NDErs and their growing awareness that they are the Light, I understand that I, too, am this Light and that we are all one. This means that I am one with those who have gone on to the other side in a way that goes far beyond what I was taught as a child. Communication between the two worlds is constant and instantaneous, and so I am never alone.

For example, recently I was in tropical Florida with its lush orange groves and trees draped in Spanish moss. I longed to share this with my father, who as a former farmer was enchanted with every plant. I wished he were there with me. Then I realized that my dad is the same Light that is me, and that he really was with me, admiring the same trees I was seeing. While he was alive, whenever we drove through the Midwest together, he would find something to admire where I only saw a corn field.

So, I asked my dad to show me what most delighted him. I had a sense that he was saying, "Did you see that eagle?" I thought, "This is crazy! Eagles aren't a tropical bird, and I've never heard of one in Florida." Nevertheless, I searched and there he was—in an oak tree. As soon as I noticed him, he started to flap his wings as if ready to fly away in fear. So I looked at him and consciously held the awareness that we were one in our shared loving Light. His fear seemed to vanish, and he allowed me to approach until I was within about fifty feet of him. We admired each other, and my sense of our connection grew even greater, until I felt as if I were the eagle. I sensed he wanted to fly home. I told him he could, and off he flew. It seemed to me that my father was smiling and that he had given me his eyes that always saw the surprise in the corn field.

Remembering That I Am Light

For me (Denny), the most moving aspect of the NDE and the one that has brought about the greatest change in my life is the revelation of who I am. This has been the culmination of a long process.

I understand this process in terms of remembering that I am the Light. As a child, I was taught that the Light was somewhere else: in a Somebody Somewhere named God, in Jesus, in the Eucharist, in the priest, and so forth. Anywhere but in me. I became a religious addict, compulsively observing religious practices in a desperate effort to reach and hold onto this Light that would save me from hell. I entered the Jesuit religious order at the age of 17, because the Jesuits had the longest training of any order and I thought I needed all the help I could get. Soon after entering, I made the general confession of my life mentioned in Chapter 12. This was healing, but now I believe it was not because I was granted some sort of divine forgiveness, but rather because the priest saw and affirmed my goodness—my Light— and I gained a glimpse of myself. However, for years thereafter, although I grew and was healed in many ways, I continued to believe and to teach that the Light was something external to myself that, at best, could come and fill me.

The biggest shift in me came around the time that Sheila's and my son John was born. Two things converged at that time. One is that we were reading books about NDEs for a part of a chapter in the book we were then writing. At the same time, in preparation for John's birth, we were attending a training program in pre- and perinatal psychology. Our studies in this field were highly experiential, and included many experiences of regressing to this period of our lives, even all the way back to conception.[1]

I had known that my birth was breech; that is, I was positioned to come out feet first. My mother had told me that I was born on Thanksgiving Day at 10:00 p.m. (She made quite a point of saying that she wished she hadn't eaten such a big Thanksgiving dinner before she went to the hospital. . . .) At the hospital, my father was told that the birth had been very difficult, I was not doing well, and I might not survive. The next morning at 2:00 a.m., the doctors finally filled out my birth certificate and gave my birth date as Friday, the day after Thanksgiving. Evidently, it was only then that they believed I was going to live.

During several regressions, I re-experienced not only my birth but also my prenatal life going all the way back to conception. What became evident to me was that I did not want to leave the world I had come from. Even the positioning of my body indicated this, as if my arms were reaching back, trying to return. I am reminded of the stories of many NDErs, who report that they did not want to leave the next life and return to this one. I did not want to be born because I was afraid that in this world I would forget the Light that I am. I did forget . . . for a while.

All of this happened around the time that John was born, and it was the beginning of a journey of remembering. As Sheila and I held John and looked into his eyes, we saw the Light from which he had come, and it has always been evident to us that he *is* this Light. If we had been tempted to teach him the things I was taught as a child and that turned me into a religious addict, his eyes would have stopped us. John knew where he came from, and we realized that our primary responsibility as his parents is to shelter him from anything that might try to make him forget.

The psychiatrist Joan Fitzherbert speaks of children under the age of two as having one foot in this world and the other still in the world of Light from which they came.[2] This was certainly my experience of my breech birth, although in my case it was both my hands that were reaching back for the Light. John is all here now with both feet on the ground and both hands fully engaged with the world around him, but at seventeen he still remembers far more than I did at his age of where he comes from and who he is.

As I have looked into John's eyes since he was a newborn, I too have remembered. Then, in recent years as we have focused more intensely on NDEs with the intention of catching the benign virus, these two experiences have come together. The place we come from, as John has revealed it to me, and the place we are going, as NDErs have described it, are one and the same: a world of love and Light. And the lesson of both is that we are this love and Light. During the life review, one NDEr experienced "being inside my mother and then I was this pure light. I was part of everything and everything was part of me."[3] Consider the following story that our friend, Karen, shared with us about her granddaughter, Sarah.

Karen and her daughter and son-in-law, Emily and Steve, were on vacation at a resort. At 3:00 a.m., Emily and Steve, faces ashen, knocked on Karen's door. They asked Karen if the lights had gone on in her room. Karen said, "No. What's wrong?" Emily and Steve explained they were awakened by the feeling of someone running across the bed. At first, each thought the other was getting up. At the same moment, all the lights went on in the room. The lights were on separate switches, which meant that someone would have had to go from one switch to another to turn them all on at once. As Karen, Emily, and Steve talked about this, Emily sensed that she had conceived a child. Sure enough, Sarah was born nine months later.

Two years after Sarah's birth, the whole family (including Sarah) was together in Karen's kitchen. They recalled the resort vacation. Sarah said, "I remember that place." Her mother said, "How can you remember it? You weren't born yet." Sarah answered, "I was there. Don't you remember? I ran across your bed." No one had ever mentioned to Sarah what had awoken Emily and Steve that night, yet Sarah apparently remembered her eagerness to be their child. Two years later, Sarah again referred to the night of her conception. She said, "I was light and I wanted to put more light into the room." (Note that, at its best, conception is a joyful union of egg and sperm in a biochemical explosion of light.[4])

This Light, so evident in the eyes of our newborn John, is the same Light we saw in Ralph's eyes following his NDE. (See Chapter 1.) Ralph, too, has one foot in this world and the other in the next world, which is the same world he and all of us originally came from. Babies remind us of this world and so do NDErs. Both have helped me to remember who I am. I no longer need to look elsewhere for the Light. Everything I was looking for is inside myself. As we quoted Ken Ring earlier, "There is an essential teaching from the Light that, NDErs say, applies to everyone. . . . It wants you to realize that your core being is this Light—it is not something external to you."[5]

Healing Process

1. Close your eyes and put your feet flat on the floor. Breathe slowly and deeply. Place your hand on your heart and imagine that you are breathing in and out through your heart. With each breath, let your awareness grow that you are Light and love.

2. Let yourself reflect back upon the stories and commentaries regarding NDEs that we have shared thus far. Ask yourself what aspect of the NDE moves or attracts you most.

3. Is there any way in which this has already changed or might change your life? In other words, have you begun to catch the benign virus, and if so what "symptoms" do you notice?

Reflection Questions

What touched me most in this chapter is . . .

When I reflect upon this chapter in relation to my life, I feel . . . I want . . .

⇜ 18 ⇝

Already Home: We Come from Where We Are Going

The worlds above this one flow with emotion, with warmth that is more than simply physical, and with other qualities far above and beyond my ability to describe. But I can tell you this: I was ready for them. Though they struck me with a dazzling newness and freshness, they were also, paradoxically familiar. I'd felt them before. Not as Eben Alexander, but as the spiritual being I was long, long before that particular embodied being came along, and that I will be again, when the earthly elements that currently make up my physical body have gone their different ways.

—Eben Alexander[1]

For me (Sheila), like Denny, the most moving aspect of immersing myself in NDEs has also been remembering who I am, but in a somewhat different way because I lost contact with my essential self for different reasons. I was never taught to find the Light outside myself as Denny was; I was never taught about Light at all. The side of my family that I grew up with were observant Jews, with an emphasis on ritual practices but little or no mention of any reality beyond the material world around us.

I always knew that I had come from the Light, that I was that Light, and that everything else was Light as well. I could see it radiating from everything and everyone around me. It was evident to me that my extended family were good and well-meaning people, and I could see their Light. However, they carried the scars of anti-Semitism from centuries of persecution in Europe. They found a safe haven in America, and, by the time I was born, most of them had achieved considerable success here. Economic security for themselves and their children was, as far as I could tell, the focus of their lives.

In contrast, I always knew I came from somewhere else and that it was a wonderful, radiant world of infinite goodness. Although I do not like the "up there" connotation of the word, I remembered "heaven." However, there was not a single member of my family with whom I could have shared this and who could have reflected back to me my deepest self. So, my mirror was the natural world. It was the Light in trees, plants, flowers, blades of grass, and so forth that reflected back to me who I was. With the help of these living beings, the inner depth of my self was preserved, but in the outer world I was extremely shy, frightened and withdrawn. It was as if the unique way in which my true self wanted to radiate the Light that I am was buried deep within. The outer expression of my personality was frozen gray.

Remembering the Colors of My Light

As a human, embedded in a social world, I needed human mirrors in order to be myself in that world. Looking back, I see that eventually I went . . . or was led . . . from one person or group of people to another, all of them in touch with the Light of a world beyond material reality. In high school, my psychology teacher saw who I was and she brought me theology books. She was Jewish, like my family, but with an openness to a larger world that I could not find at home. Then I went to Duke University, where I initially majored in psychology. It was taught in quite an empirical, materialistic way that seemed to lack contact with the Light, and so I transferred to the religion department. I knew I was in the right place there, and that spirituality was my home. So, when I graduated from Duke, I went to seminary at the Graduate Theological Union in Berkeley. There, I sought out teachers who seemed to have an especially acute sense of the Light and, most importantly, who saw it in me and who loved me. They were my mirrors.

When I finished school, I began to work in pastoral ministry, writing books and giving retreats with Denny and Matt. I knew when I first met Denny that I had known him from long before, and so we married. I knew we had a child coming to us, that his name was John, and that he had always been ours. Together, Denny and I kept exploring one thing after another with Matt that helped us both remember our Light. Each new learning seemed to come to us as a free gift and at exactly the right moment, as if an inner knowing was guiding the whole process and reminding us of who we are and where we come from. My life here matches my life there in many ways now, as if something deep within me never forgot and knew intuitively how to recreate the home I came from. Catching the NDE virus has been a confirmation of what I knew as a small child, no matter how deeply buried it was within me.

The Two Worlds Are the Same

The world I remember from which I came and the world to which I am going are the same place. These two worlds intersect in stories of NDErs whose life review takes them back through the womb to before they were born and in stories of NDErs who encounter the children who are coming to them. Following is an example, recounted by Debbie, who had an NDE following a violent assault when she was five years old. She reports the following conversation with a being of Light, who said:

"Your body has died too soon. . . . You have not completed your mission on earth. You need to go back."

I cried, "I want to stay here. Why can't I stay here? What did I do wrong?"

"You did nothing wrong. You are innocent. You need to raise your children," he calmly stated.

"It doesn't make any sense. I don't have any kids. I'm only five years old!"

He responded with the persistence of a loving parent. "That is why you need to return. When you grow up you will have children."

After taking Debbie on a journey through space and time and into a realm that Debbie says "did not have light shining on it, it was light!" the being said,

"There is someone I want you to meet." . . . That is when I saw them. Four ethereal beings were before me. They had the same translucent beauty to them as everything else I had seen. Something deep inside me stirred and I recognized my children-to-be . . .

. . . The first one touched my arm and communicated through his touch as well as telepathically. Andrew was anxious to be born on earth. I explained to him that someone else could be his mother and that it might be better for him anyway. He was insistent that he and his siblings wanted only me. If I did not go back it would frustrate plans and commitments we made with each other before I was born. I could not dissuade him. The other three were also trying to convince me that I should return because time was running out. . . .

I could not understand their insistence that only I could be their earthly mother, nor could I comprehend how I was to even live

long enough to accomplish it because of the abuse I endured on earth. I just knew that I had been told that I would. These four magnificent beings wanted me to be their mother and I could not deny them.

My friend touched my elbow drawing my attention away from my unborn children. "You must choose now."

"Isn't there another way?"

"Not if you want to fulfill the commitments you made with your children and others before you were born . . ."

. . . With new understanding I said, "I will go. . . ."

. . . I felt myself being drawn through a funnel of swirling energy toward Earth. The next thing I knew, I was back in my body.

Debbie believes that the love she experienced during her NDE kept her alive despite repeated abuse. As an adult, she gave birth to the four children she met during her NDE and has lovingly raised them. Describing her life now, she says, "These children are the spirits that I met when I was five years old. They are the light and joy of my life." Debbie and her children have broken the cycle of abuse and given future generations of children in their family line the opportunity to grow up in safety and peace.[2]

We Come from the World of NDEs

The preceding story of Debbie's NDE is also an example of what is known as a "pre-birth experience," meaning experiencing our own life before conception or encountering those who have yet to be born. Pre-birth experiences may have many of the same elements as NDEs, such as intense love, a brilliant yet peaceful light, being out of one's body, feeling connected to everything, universal knowledge, meeting loved ones, and a reluctance to leave that gives way to a willingness to fulfill one's purpose on earth. In NDEs, a trusted figure often accompanies the experiencer at least partway back into his or her body; similarly, in pre-birth experiences, a trusted figure may accompany the person into a physical form.[3] Moreover, a pre-birth experience provides a kind of template for the rest of life, as does an NDE—a template of love and meaning.

In Chapter 2, we described a visit by Virginia, an NDEr, to one of Ken Ring's classes, and the envious reaction of his students. Many of us might wish we could visit the world experienced by NDErs, especially if we could avoid the physical suffering that often precedes such an experience. However, what has become clear to us is that we have already visited that world; even more, it is the world from which we come, and we all have the capacity to remember it. As Debbie said,

> The longer I stayed, the more familiar this place felt. Feelings of homesickness enveloped me. I began to comprehend that I came from here. This was the place I lived before I went to earth. I had come home.[4]

Healing Process

1. Close your eyes and put your feet flat on the floor. Breathe slowly and deeply. Place your hand on your heart and imagine that you are breathing in and out through your heart. With each breath, let your awareness grow that you are Light and love.

2. As you reflect on your life, is there anyone with whom you have a feeling of profound connection and rightness, comparable to Debbie's sense of connection with her four children in the story above?

3. For example, do you have a relationship with anyone with whom you feel as if you may have known that person forever and that your relationship may be part of the reason you came here?

4. Or, is there an aspect of your life, such as Debbie's calling to stop the cycle of abuse in her family line or Peggy's calling to sing (see Chapter 13), in which you feel as if you are doing exactly what you came here to do?

5. Whatever you get in touch with, hold this quality of connection and rightness in your heart and let it grow there. Notice if anything comes to you in terms of the meaning of this relationship or aspect of your life.

6. If you wish, imagine yourself in the world from which you came, before you were born. Imagine that you are being sent here. Listen for anything you might have been told about this relationship or aspect of your life.

Reflection Questions

What touched me most in this chapter is . . .

When I reflect upon this chapter in relation to my life, I feel . . . I want . . .

~ 19 ~

The Universal Donor

What I love about NDEs . . . is that their religious and spiritual implications are so inclusive and universalistic. NDEs are the type O blood in the discourse on spirituality—the equivalent of the universal donor.[1]

—Kenneth Ring

All three of us are introverts, and parties or other social gatherings can be an ordeal for us. Our usual strategy is to find at least one person we know well and stay near that person. Since we began writing this book, we have found ourselves walking into a room full of people and discovering that we could have a meaningful conversation with anyone there. As soon as someone asks us what we are doing currently, and we tell them we are reading and writing about near-death experiences, their eyes widen, their attention seems to focus, and they start asking questions. Almost always, they know someone who has had an NDE, and surprisingly often they have had one themselves. Even the skeptics seem fascinated.

We (Denny and Sheila) live in a community in which many people have different political opinions, values, religious beliefs, and lifestyles than ourselves. The rewards of learning to play musical chairs skillfully are evident in the affluence of many of our neighbors, as well as the pressures to continue doing so. However, as soon as the conversation turns to NDEs, political and socioeconomic differences fade away. We seem to be drawn together by what Raymond Moody, quoted in the Introduction, describes as the attraction of NDEs:

> . . . hearing about them triggers a memory deep within us. It is sort of like a homecoming. Accounts of NDEs are like echoes that resonate from somewhere inside ourselves so that we want to keep hearing stories that awaken us more fully to that awareness.[2]

In our experience, NDEs have the power to unite us as no other topic can, and to help us form immediate heart and soul connections with people to whom we might otherwise struggle to relate.

A dramatic example for us is the memorial service that we (Denny and Sheila) celebrated for Zeke. It was held at the school that Zeke attended with our son John. It is an independent school, with no religious affiliation. We wondered how we could possibly represent Zeke's family, who resonate to Native American spirituality, and still speak to our audience of one thousand people that included Christian fundamentalists, conservative Catholics, Jews, Buddhists, atheists, and everything in between. We guessed that the best we could do was tell them what had helped Zeke's family when we were with them in the hospital, in hopes that it would help them, too. We spoke about the evidence from NDEs and his family's own experience that Zeke is just fine and remains very near to us. It is we who miss him who need healing of our grief, we said, and Zeke will find ways to help us.

Based on the feedback, we seem to have guessed right about how to speak to this group. We felt especially moved by comments from the parents of Zeke's classmates, who told us how comforted their children were by hearing that Zeke is still with them, and how right this sounded to them. John tells us, "All the kids at school think you're really cool! It's because of the memorial service." We think what they are trying to say is that we gave them permission to trust a kind of knowing that they still have. They remember where they came from, even though our culture encourages them to forget.

Perhaps the memorial service opened a door and made it okay to be open to experiences of Zeke's presence and share them. As people have shared such experiences with Zeke's family, these stories have added to the family's awareness of Zeke, as if he is building up a kind of buffer or container of comfort around them to help them grieve without despairing.

Yesterday we (Denny and Sheila) went out for a walk. A woman we did not know stopped us and said, with tears in her eyes,

> You're the ones who did the service for Zeke, aren't you? My children went to his school and I've known the family for years. That was the most hopeful memorial service I've ever been to. Thank you.

We have lived in our town for twenty-four years, and she has lived here for forty years. Her dog-walking route and our jogging route overlap, and we have passed each other many times. We had never had a conversation with her before, but within two minutes we felt a deep heart connection with her. The credit for her experience of the memorial service does not go to us; all we did was hold the community's grief in the Light of Zeke's ongoing presence. The credit goes to the universal power and appeal of NDEs, and how they remind us that the door between this world and the next is open. We all know this because deep within we remember the world from which we came, and this is the same world to which we will return. Death and NDEs can draw us together and hold us together because they remind us of our common origin and our common destiny. They remind us that we are already home.

Near-Death Experiences Transcend Divisions

We have come to believe that near-death experiences transcend all our usual categories of human division, and the research supports this. They happen to people of all cultures, races, religions, socioeconomic strata, levels of education, and ages. Across all these divisions, the elements of an NDE are basically the same.

All humans and all creation are loved infinitely and equally; no person is of greater value than another, and no one is lost. Although humans have fought religious wars for millennia, NDErs consistently report that one's religion, or whether one adheres to any religion, does not matter. All that matters is that we live according to the most fundamental teaching of all religions, which is the primacy of love. Perhaps this is why so many NDErs lose interest in formal religion, even as they devote themselves to spiritual growth.[3]

NDEs also transcend the usual barriers in interpersonal relationships, in that "all previous filters that may have screened you off from yourself and others are removed."[4] In other words, the psychological defenses and limitations of human communication that normally may make it difficult for us to fully understand ourselves and one another are gone. We see ourselves and others with absolute clarity. In this environment of perfect transparency, during the life review NDErs often experience their life from the point of view of every person they ever interacted with. They also know everything about those other people. For example, in the story of Tom Sawyer (see Chapter 12), he not only felt the thirty-two blows he inflicted on the pedestrian he hit, but he also "experienced unbelievable things about that man that are of a very personal, confidential, and private nature."[5]

Near-death experiences transcend the differences and separations between human beings because they reveal the essence of the self underlying all divisions. As Anita Moorjani describes it,

> Here I am without my body, race, culture, religion or beliefs . . . yet I continue to exist! . . . I was enveloped in the oneness, the pure essence of every living being and creature, without their aches, pains, dramas and egos. . . .
>
> I became aware that we're all connected. This was not only every person and living creature, but the interwoven unification felt as though it were expanding outward to include everything in the universe—every human, animal, plant, insect, mountain, sea, inanimate object, and the cosmos. . . . We're all facets of that unity—we're all One. . . .[6]

Love Is the Glue

The glue of our oneness is love. NDEs remind us that we are made of love; they transcend religion because they are based upon what is already written in our hearts. All humans long for love and are happiest when they are in touch with their essence and therefore in a conscious state of love. As Kenneth Ring puts it, "And what is love? It's caring, it's compassion, and the realization that we are all connected at the deepest level as one being".[7]

Because the message of the NDE is based on our essential nature, it has the power to unite humanity:

> Unlike spiritual paths that arose from the ideas and inner experiences of lone, isolated human beings, the path presented by near-death experiences is emerging as a direct, grassroots revelation

that millions of people from all over the world are receiving and sharing. If we explore this newly emerging path deeply enough, we discover that all religions, philosophies, and cultures are honored; that science and spirituality are celebrated; that both the human and spiritual side of our natures are embraced as beautiful and essential. In short, near-death experiences present us with a universal, all-inclusive, perfectly integrated spiritual path that revolves around three core truths: 1. We are all one; 2. Love is the essence of life; 3. We are here, in this world, to become perfect embodiments of the divine.[8]

Many people believe that humanity is at a crossroads, on the brink of a significant transformation in consciousness. Multiple sources are feeding this transformation; the near-death experience is one of them. P. M. H. Atwater writes,

. . . a study done in the United States, and released in 2009 reported that 49 percent of the population had undergone a sudden awakening—through a near-death state or because of a transcendent, mystical, religious or spiritual experience—that completely changed the way they viewed life. . . . After effects were said to be continuous, as if making new choices based on a new vision was enough to start the process of becoming new.[9]

As increasing numbers of people have NDEs and communicate their experiences, the unitive power of the NDE may help us reach the tipping point of the transformation in human consciousness that so many of us believe is coming.

Reflecting on his own NDE, Mellen-Thomas Benedict writes,

In one of my visits with the Light I was told that the near-death experience . . . would become more and more popular and it would have an effect on the entire world when a critical mass was

*hit and all these people have died and come back and are telling
you that there is a lot more going on than we think. . . .*

*Everyone has direct access. Everyone is directly connected to The
Source that we all are. There are many ways to get there. . . . It
is as natural as breathing, as natural as sunlight. What we have
to realize is that we all have that direct connection. Some can do
it through meditation. Some through song and dance. There is
[sic] a million ways to do it. And no one is ever cut off.*[10]

Catching and Living the Benign Virus: The Golden Rule

As we wait in hope for the transformation of our world, the
NDE can teach us how to live now so that we both help bring
about that transformation and are ready for it when it comes.
The core teaching of all religions as to how we should live can
be summarized in the Golden Rule: Do unto others as you would
have them do unto you. Although we have all heard this, few
of us have grasped the literal truth of it. When we die, we will
relive everything we have done to others as they experienced
it. We will feel the happiness of those to whom we were kind
and loving, and the suffering of those to whom we were unkind
and unloving. Whatever we do to others, we literally do it to
ourselves. "There is really only one person in the universe—and
that person is, of course, yourself."[11]

If we take this seriously, we will live every moment with the
intention of bringing the same joy to others that we wish for
ourselves. Ultimately, the same thing makes all humans happy:
being treated with love and kindness. We all know this for ourselves, and we have only to do it for others.

*To dwell on the nature of the afterlife may divert us from paying
attention to THIS life, where the lessons from the Light need to
be practiced. . . . The true promise of the NDE is not so much
what it suggests about an afterlife—as inspiring and comforting*

*as those glimpses are—but what it says about how to live NOW
. . . to learn from NDErs about how to live, or how to live better, with greater self-awareness, self-compassion, and concern
for others. Live well, and death will take care of itself."*[12]

Healing Process

1. Close your eyes and put your feet flat on the floor. Breathe
    slowly and deeply. Place your hand on your heart and imagine
    that you are breathing in and out through your heart. With
    each breath, let your awareness grow that you are love.

2. Imagine that you have had a near-death experience, of the
    kind that sometimes happens when one is not in actual
    danger of death. Perhaps you were walking in nature, per-
    haps you were sitting quietly and meditating or praying,
    perhaps you were watching a sunset, and so forth. Whatever
    the context, you found yourself in the realm of infinite,
    unconditional love described in this book. All the hurts of
    your life and all your self-doubts were transcended, and you
    were filled with the awareness that your essence is Light and
    love. You also realized that whatever you do to another, you
    are really doing to yourself. Imagine yourself returning from
    such an experience and going to sleep resting in a sense of
    perfect peace.

3. When you woke up the next morning, how would you live
    that day? What would you do the same? What would you do
    differently?

Reflection Questions

What touched me most in this chapter is . . .

When I reflect upon this chapter in relation to my life,
I feel . . . I want . . .

Appendix A

Elements of a Near-Death Experience

According to Raymond Moody:

1. *The ineffability of the experience.*

2. *A feeling of peace and quiet; pain is gone.*

3. *The awareness of being dead, sometimes followed by a noise.*

4. *An out-of-body experience (OBE); from a position outside and above their bodies, people witness their own resuscitation or operation.*

5. *A dark space, experienced by only 15 percent of people as [initially] frightening; people are pulled toward a small pinpoint of light in this dark space, which they describe as:*

   • *A tunnel experience; they are drawn rapidly toward the light.*

   • *A frightening NDE; approximately 1 to 2 percent of people [who have NDEs] linger in this dark space and experience their NDE as frightening.*

6. *The perception of an unearthly environment, a dazzling landscape with beautiful colors, gorgeous flowers, and sometimes also music.*

7. Meeting and communicating with deceased persons, mostly relatives.

8. Seeing a brilliant light or a being of light; experiencing complete acceptance and unconditional love and gaining access to a deep knowledge and wisdom.

9. The panoramic life review, or review of life from birth: people see their entire life flash before them; there appears to be no time or distance, everything happens at once, and people can talk for days about a life review that lasted only a few minutes.

10. The preview or flash forward: people have the impression that they are witness to part of the life that is yet to come; again there is no time or distance.

11. The perception of a border: people are aware that if they cross this border or limit they will never be able to return to their body.

12. The conscious return to the body, accompanied by great disappointment at having something so beautiful taken away.[1]

Appendix B

Frequency of Near-Death Stages

According to *Evidence of the Afterlife,* by Jeffrey Long, no two near-death experiences are identical.[1] When, however, many near-death experiences are studied, a common pattern of elements emerges, which usually occur in consistent order. Here is a list of the twelve main NDE elements that have been identified. Each element is followed by a number indicating what percentage of the 613 people included in the *Evidence of the Afterlife* study experienced the element in question.

1. Out-of-body experience (OBE): Separation of consciousness from the physical body—75.4 percent

2. Heightened senses—74.4 percent

3. Intense and generally positive emotions or feelings—76.2 percent

4. Passing into or through a tunnel—33.8 percent

5. Encountering a mystical or brilliant light—64.6 percent

6. Encountering other beings, either mystical beings or deceased relatives or friends—57.3 percent

7. A sense of alteration of time and space—60.5 percent

8. Life review—22.2 percent

9. Encountering unworldly ("heavenly") realms—40.6 percent

10. Encountering or learning special knowledge—56 percent
    (31.5 percent answered that they felt they understood every-
    thing "about the universe"; 31.3 percent felt they under-
    stood everything "about myself and others.")

11. Encountering a boundary or barrier—31 percent

12. Return to the body, either voluntary or involuntary—58.5
    percent

The Gifts of Near-Death Experiences

Appendix C

Life Changes After a Cardiac Arrest
With and Without an NDE

In his prospective study of NDEs, cardiologist Pim van Lommel and his colleagues interviewed cardiac arrest patients five days later, two years later, and eight years later. Van Lommel summarizes the long-term changes as follows:

> . . . *after eight years, people with an NDE scored significantly higher in the following areas: showing emotions; less interest in the opinion of others; accepting others; compassion for others; involvement in family; less appreciation of money and possessions; increase in the importance of nature and the environment; less interest in a higher standard of living; appreciation of ordinary things; sense of social justice; inner meaning of life; decline in church attendance; increased interest in spirituality; less fear of death; less fear of dying; and increase in belief in life after death. These different levels of change are a consequence of the NDE and not of surviving a cardiac arrest.*[1]

Note that in the following chart summarizing his findings, van Lommel is comparing cardiac arrest patients who had an NDE with those who did not, which means, as Van Lommel says above, that the changes cannot be attributed to the cardiac arrest itself.

The figures in the chart reflect the percentage of people indicating a slight to strong increase in the extent to which they had changed. A negative percentage indicates a decrease.

From Pim van Lommel, *Consciousness Beyond Life: The Science of the Near-Death Experience* (New York: HarperCollins, 2010), 68.

	Increase (percent)		Increase (percent)	
	Cardiac Arrest with NDE		*Cardiac Arrest without NDE*	
	At 8 years	**At 2 years**	**At 8 years**	**At 2 years**
Understanding oneself	58	63	8	58
Positive outlook on future	26	57	58	50
Understand purpose of life	52	63	25	50
Showing emotions	42	78	16	58
Wanting to help others	26	73	8	58
Opinion of others	–31	–21	8	41
Listening to others	47	52	8	75
Accepting others	42	78	16	41
Showing love	52	68	25	50
Compassion for others	47	73	41	50
Empathy with others	36	73	8	75
Involvement in family	47	78	33	58

The Gifts of Near-Death Experiences

Interest in meaning of life	52	89	33	66
Appreciation of money and possessions	47	−42	−25	−25
Importance of nature and environment	47	84	33	58
Importance of higher standard of living	−25	−50	0	33
Appreciation of ordinary things	78	84	41	50
Sense of social justice	75	68	16	33
What matters in life	42	57	33	66
Meaning of faith	52	57	33	66
Sense inner meaning of life	52	57	25	25
Religious beliefs	36	47	16	25
Church attendance	−15	−42	8	25
Interest in spirituality	15	42	−8	−41
Interest in death	21	47	8	8
Fear of death	−47	−63	−16	−41
Fear of dying	−26	−47	−16	−25
Belief in life after death	36	42	16	16

Appendix D

Gifts of Near-Death Experiences
Free Online Video Stories Seminar

Following is a suggested format for a seminar based on this book and on over forty online NDE video stories. This is the same basic format that is used for our other seminars that are based on our books. It is simple, requires no training, and has been used by thousands of people all over the world. You can take this seminar by yourself, with one other companion, or with a group. Feel free to adapt the suggested format accordingly.

If you share the seminar with one or more other people, meetings may be held once each week or scheduled according to the needs of the group. For example, several sessions could be scheduled on one whole day or over a weekend. The length of each part of the meeting can be adapted as needed.

Prior to Each Meeting:

Read that week's chapter in this book.

During Each Meeting:

1. Quiet time to get in touch with what moved you the most during the past week, including what you read in this week's chapter (five minutes).

2. Sharing in twos: What moved you the most? (ten minutes).

3. Watch one or more of the short videos that accompany this week's chapter, available at *www.linnministries.org* (approximately five to twenty minutes).

4. Silent Reflection: Quiet time to get in touch with what moved you most deeply in the video(s) (five minutes).

5. Healing Process: Do the process at the end of this week's chapter (ten minutes).

6. Sharing in twos: What has moved you the most during this session? (five minutes).

7. Group Sharing: Share whatever has touched you most during this meeting or in this week's chapter. You may wish to include how immersing yourself in this material is affecting your life. (twenty minutes).

8. Closing snack and celebration.

The Gifts of Near-Death Experiences

Suggested Resources on Near-Death Experiences

Books

Chris Carter, *Science and the Near-Death Experience: How Consciousness Survives Death* (Rochester, VT: Inner Traditions, 2010).

Jeffrey Long, *Evidence of the Afterlife: The Science of Near-Death Experiences* (New York: HarperCollins, 2010).

Raymond Moody, *Glimpses of Eternity: Sharing a Loved One's Passage from This Life to the Next* (New York: Guideposts, 2010).

Anita Moorjani, *Dying to Be Me: My Journey from Cancer, to Near Death, to True Healing* (New York: Hay House, 2012).

Kenneth Ring, *Lessons from the Light: What We Can Learn from the Near-Death Experience* (Needham, MA: Moment Point Press, 2006).

Pim van Lommel, *Consciousness Beyond Life: The Science of the Near-Death Experience* (New York: HarperCollins, 2010).

Websites

www.nderf.org: Dr. Jeffrey and Jody Long's site, summarizing their research. Includes thousands of NDE accounts from all over the world.

www.near-death.com: Kevin Williams's site, summarizing the research on major NDE topics.

www.iands.org: International Association of Near-Death Studies index to NDE literature, 1877–2011.

Endnotes

Introduction: Catching the Benign Virus

1. P. M. H. Atwater, *Beyond the Light* (New York: Birch Lane Press, 1994), 49–50.

2. Raymond Moody, *Life After Life* (New York: HarperCollins, 1975).

3. Raymond Moody, *The Light Beyond* (New York: Bantam, 1989), 150.

4. Interview with Jeffrey Long, "Is There Life After Death?—Scientific Research Facts," *https://www.youtube.com/watch?v=7HhOZLN_9FM* (accessed May 31, 2015). NDE accounts may be accessed at Jeffrey and Jody Long's website, *www.nderf.org*

5. Long, 149, 171; J. Steve Miller, *Near-Death Experiences* (Lexington, KY: Wisdom Creek Press, 2013), 98–100; Pim van Lommel, *Consciousness Beyond Life: The Science of the Near-Death Experience* (New York: HarperCollins, 2010), 110.

Some researchers have suggested that the NDEs of non-Westerners rarely if ever include life reviews. See, for example, Masayuki Ohkado and Bruce Greyson, "A Comparative Analysis of Japanese and Western NDEs," *Journal of Near-Death Studies* 32(4), Summer, 2014, 187–198. Dr. Jeffrey Long argues that the samples used for these studies are too small, and maintains that his study of what are now thousands of NDEs from all over the world indicates that they are basically similar in all cultures. Long writes, "Directly comparing the elements of non-Western and Western near-death experiences revealed that all elements that occurred in Western NDEs were found in non-Western NDEs as well." Long, 170.

6. Raymond Moody, *Glimpses of Eternity: Sharing a Loved One's Passage from This Life to the Next* (New York: Guideposts, 2010), 49. Includes many accounts of shared death experiences (SDEs).

7. Moody, *Glimpses of Eternity*, 50.

8. Nancy Clark, *Divine Moments: Ordinary People Having Spiritually Transformative Experiences* (Fairfield , IA: 1st World Publishing, 2012).

9. Interview with Jeffrey Long, "Is There Life After Death— Scientific Research Facts," *https://www.youtube.com/ watch?v=7HhOZLN_9FM* (accessed May 31, 2015).

10. *http://www.nderf.org/NEDRF/Research/number_nde_usa.htm* (accessed August 5, 2012).

11. *http://www.youtube.com/watch?v=pgBdf1GqNIA* (accessed January 10, 2014).

12. Kenneth Ring, personal correspondence, April 22, 2014.

13. Idem.

14. Kenneth Ring, *Lessons from the Light: What We Can Learn from the Near-Death Experience* (Needham, MA: Moment Point Press, 2006), xii.

15. Ring, *Lessons from the Light*.

16. Ibid., 3–4; Janice Miner Holden, Bruce Greyson and Debbie James, *The Handbook of Near-Death Experiences: Thirty Years of Investigation* (Denver: Praeger Publishers, 2009), 252–253; Lynne McTaggart, *The Bond: Connecting through the Space Between Us* (New York: Free Press, 2011), 92–93.

17. Jeffrey Long, *Evidence of the Afterlife: The Science of Near-Death Experiences* (New York: HarperCollins, 2010), 202.

Chapter 1: Musical Chairs: Remembering Our Home

1. Terry Orlick, *The Cooperative Sports and Games Book* (New York: Pantheon, 1978).

2. Aldous Huxley, Introduction to Sisirkumar Ghose, *Mystics as a Force for Change* (Wheaton, IL: Theosophical Publishing House, Quest Books, 1981), cited in Cherie Sutherland, *Reborn in the Light: Life After Near-Death Experiences* (New York: Bantam, 1992), 190–191.

3. van Lommel, *Consciousness Beyond Life*, 68.

4. According to hospice nurse Bronnie Ware, the top five regrets of dying patients are (1) "I wish I'd had the courage to live a life true to myself, not the life others expected of me." (2) "I wish I hadn't worked so hard." (3) "I wish I'd had the courage to express my feelings." (4) "I wish I had stayed in touch with my friends." (5) "I wish that I had let myself be happier." Susie Steiner, "Top Five Regrets of the Dying," *www.theguardian.com*, February 1, 2012. Based on Bronnie Ware, *The Top Five Regrets of the Dying* (Carlsbad, CA: Hay House, 2012).

5. Kenneth Ring, personal correspondence, September 1, 2013.

6. Long, *Evidence of the Afterlife*, 3.

7. van Lommel, *Consciousness Beyond Life*, 67–68.

8. P. M. H. Atwater, *Near-Death Experiences: The Rest of the Story* (Charlottesville, VA: Hampton Roads, 2011), 73.

Chapter 2: Beyond Words: Ineffability, Peace and Love

1. Raymond Moody, *Reflections on Life After Life* (Harrisburg, PA: Stackpole Books, 1977), 24.

2. Ring, *Lessons from the Light*, 21.

3. Kenneth Ring, *Heading Toward Omega* (New York: William Morrow, 1985), 61–62.

4. Long, *Evidence of the Afterlife*, 8.

5. Kenneth Ring, *Life at Death: A Scientific Investigation of the Near-Death Experience* (New York: Coward, McCann and Geoghegan, 1980 and Quill, 1982), 41.

6. Juriaan Kamp, "A Change of Heart Changes Everything," *Ode* (June, 2005), 22–27.

7. L. Song, G. Schwartz, and L. Russek, "Heart-Focused Attention and Heart-Brain Synchronization: Energetic and Physiological Mechanisms," *Alternative Therapies in Health and Medicine*, Vol. 4, No. 5 (1998), 44–62, cited in Doc Childre and Howard Martin, *The HeartMath Solution* (San Francisco: Harper, 1999), 33. See also *www.heartmath.org/research*.

8. Childre and Martin, *The HeartMath Solution*, 28–34, ff. See also *www.heartmath.org/research*.

9. Childre and Martin, *The HeartMath Solution*, 33–34; Kamp, "A Change of Heart Changes Everything," 22–27. See also *www.heartmath.org/research*.

10. See *www.heartmath.org/research*. For research on treating ADD/ADHD in children, see Shari St. Martin, Biofeedback Clinic, Guadalajara, Jalisco, Mexico, "The Garden of the Heart: The New Biotechnology for Treating Children with ADD/ADHD and Arrhythmia," *www.heartmath.org/research/rp-garden-of-the-heart-heartmath-the-new-biotechnology-for-treating-children-with-add/adhd.html* (accessed August 28, 2010).

11. Anita Moorjani, *Dying to Be Me* (Carlsbad, CA: Hay House, 2012).

12. Moorjani, *Dying to Be Me*, 139.

13. Ring, *Lessons from the Light*, 143.

Chapter 3: Out of the Body, or We're Bigger Than We Think

1. Moody, *Glimpses of Eternity*, 60–61.

2. Atwater, *Near-Death Experiences*, 241–242.

3. Long, *Evidence of the Afterlife*, 8.

4. van Lommel, *Consciousness Beyond Life*, 19.

5. *The Day I Died*, BBC Documentary (2002), *http://www.near-death .com/experiences/evidence01.html* (accessed August 6, 2012).

6. K. Ring and M. Lawrence, "Further Evidence for Veridical Perception During Near-Death Experiences," *Journal of Near Death Studies*, 11 (1993), 225–226; David Ray Griffin, *Parapsychology, Philosophy, and Spirituality*: A Postmodern Exploration (Albany, NY: State University of New York Press, 1997), 250–251.

7. Ring and Lawrence, 226–227.

8. Ibid., 227.

9. Atwater, *Beyond the Light*, 75.

10. Atwater, *Near-Death Experiences*, *http://near-death.com /experiences/evidence10.html* (accessed December 1, 2014), 59.

11. Long, *Evidence of the* Afterlife, 76.

12. Tijn Touber, "A New Lease on Life," interview with Pim van Lommel, *http://www.theosociety.org/pasadena/sunrise/55-05-6 /de-touber.htm* (accessed May 10, 2013); originally published in *Ode*, 3(10), December, 2005. See also van Lommel, *Consciousness Beyond Life*.

13. Kenneth Ring and Sharon Cooper, *Mindsight: Near-Death and Out-of-Body Experiences in the Blind*, Second Edition (New York: iUniverse, Inc., 2008), 108, back cover.

14. Ring, *Lessons from the Light*, 75, 81. Ring found that fifteen of the twenty-one blind NDErs he studied claimed, like Vicki, to have experienced sight during their NDE. See *Mindsight*, 48.

15. C. G. Jung, *Memories, Dreams, Reflections* (New York: Vintage Books, 1965), 289–290. See also also *http://psychictruth.info/NEAR_ DEATH_EXPERIENCES.htm* (accessed August 9, 2012).

16. "Mellen-Thomas Benedict's Near-Death Experience," *http://near -death.com/experiences/reincarnation04.html* (accessed July 30, 2012), 7.

We are aware of questions that have been raised about the validity of Mellen-Thomas Benedict's account of his healing from cancer and of his NDE, as well as questions regarding his business dealings. We have consulted people who have personal knowledge of his situation, and they have assured us that his story is true. One such person is P. M. H. Atwater, a renowned near-death researcher, who saw the x-rays of Mellen-Thomas's brain that were taken before and after his NDE and is willing to attest to his healing from cancer. We have also been assured that, despite some unfortunate and unintended outcomes related to the unethical behavior of others and his own misguided trust of them, Benedict's business dealings have been well-intentioned.

17. "Seven Year Microwave Sky," can be seen at *http://map.gsfc.nasa.gov/media/101080/index.html* (accessed February 3, 2016).

18. van Lommel, *Consciousness Beyond Life*, 34–35.

19. Griffin, *Parapsychology, Philosophy, and Spirituality*, 231.

20. Leonardo Boff, "Beings of Light," *http://www.leonardoboff.com/site-eng/vista/2008/feb22.htm* (accessed August 14, 2012).

Chapter 4: Through the Tunnel: Healing Transitions

1. van Lommel, *Consciousness Beyond Life*, 27.

2. Helen, *http://near-death.com/experiences/research16.html* (accessed August 8, 2012).

3. Reinee Pasarow, *http://near-death.com/experiences/research16.html* (accessed August 8, 2013).

4. Long, *Evidence of the Afterlife*, *http://nhneneardeath.ning.com/forum/topics/book-summary-evidence-of-the-afterlife* (accessed September 1, 2013).

5. Moody, *Glimpses of Eternity*, 32–33.

6. Ring, *Lessons from the Light*, 21.

7. Rachel Naomi Remen, *Kitchen Table Wisdom* (New York: Berkeley Publishing, 1996), 311–313.

Chapter 5: Sacred Space

1. Laura M., *http://www.nderf.org/NDERF/NDE_Experiences /laura_m_ndes.htm* (accessed November 5, 2015). Punctuation and case edited by the authors.

2. Ring and Cooper, *Mindsight*, 14–16.

3. Kenneth Ring, *Heading Toward Omega: In Search of the Meaning of the Near-Death Experience* (New York: William Morrow, 1985), 176.

4. Eben Alexander with Ptolemy Tompkins, *The Map of Heaven* (New York: Simon & Schuster, 2014), 92–93.

5. Penny Sartori, "The Children Who Have Near-Death Experiences—Then Lead Charmed Lives: Study Reveals Youngsters as Young as Six Months Can Have Lucid Visions," December 4, 2014, *http://www.dailymail.co.uk/news/article-2547133/The-children -near-death-experiences-lead-charmed-lives-Study-reveals-youngsters -young-six-months-lucid-visions.html* (accessed December 4, 2014).

6. "Jan Price's Near-Death Experience with Her Pet Dog," *http:// www.near-death.com/experiences/animals01.html* (accessed September 12, 2014), 6.

7. Eruera M., *http://www.nderf.org/NDERF/eruera_ m_ nde_7053 .htm* (accessed December 14, 2014).

8. Mary Grace, *The Communion of Saints* (Phoenix: Tau Publishing, 2013), 18–19.

9. Moody, *The Light Beyond*, 42.

10. van Lommel, *Consciousness Beyond Life*, 54.

11. P. M. H. Atwater, *Beyond the Light*, 131; P. M. H. Atwater, *Coming Back to Life* (New York: Dodd, Mead & Co., 1988), 90–91, 230–231.

12. Atwater, *Beyond the Light*, 132; van Lommel, *Consciousness Beyond Life*, 59, 76.

Chapter 6: Meeting Loved Ones: People

1. Long, *Evidence of the Afterlife*, 11; E. W. Kelly, "Near-Death Experiences with Reports of Meeting Deceased People," *Death Studies* 25(2001), 229–249, cited in Long, *Evidence of the Afterlife*, 123ff.

2. Kevin Williams, "Homecoming and the Near-Death Experience," *http://www.near-death.com/experiences/research30.html* (accessed May 16, 2013).

3. Long, *Evidence of the Afterlife*, 126–127.

4. van Lommel, *Consciousness Beyond Life*, 32–33.

5. Eben Alexander, *Proof of Heaven: A Neurosurgeon's Journey into the Afterlife* (New York: Simon & Schuster, 2012), 40–41, 165–169.

6. *http://www.nderf.org/NDERF/amy_c_nde_4720.htm* (accessed December 16, 2014).

7. Moody, *The Light Beyond*, 173.

8. Kaaran Bowden, M.A. Used with permission.

9. Moody, *Glimpses of Eternity*, 159.

10. Long, *Evidence of the Afterlife*, 127–128.

Chapter 7: Meeting Loved Ones: Animals

1. Betty J. Eadie, *Embraced by the Light* (Placerville, CA: Gold Leaf Press, 1992), 38.

2. Scott S. Smith, *The Soul of Your Pet* (Edmonds, WA: Holmes Publishing Group, 2003), 88.

3. Mary R., *https://www.youtube.com/watch?v=9cXh8F5BKq0* (accessed December 16, 2014).

4. Susan, *http://www.near-death.com/experiences/christianity12.html* (accessed December 16, 2014).

5. Kim Sheridan, *Animals and the Afterlife* (Carlsbad, CA: Hay House, 2003), 194.

6. P. M. H. Atwater, *The Big Book of Near-Death Experiences* (Faber, VA: Rainbow Ridge Books, 2007), 162–163.

7. P. M. H. Atwater, *The New Children and Near-Death Experiences* (Rochester, VT: Bear & Co., 1993), 50.

8. Jan Price, *The Other Side of Death* (New York: Fawcett Columbine, 1996), 42; "Jan Price's Near-Death Experience with Her Pet Dog," 3.

9. What Jan Price describes as "pressing with her mind" seems to be the creative power that P. M. H. Atwater experienced during her NDE. P. M. H. wondered,

> . . . what would happen if I could concentrate deeply enough to bring my thoughts together into one single focus and then project that focus forward as if it were a laser beam to a specific spot in front of me. Could I purposefully solidify substance from thought alone? Could I create with it?

She decided to try creating a house, a specific house that she had in mind:

> I held my focus . . . and before me there formed an image. It happened fairly quickly and when done, I was aghast. There it was. A house. . . . This four-square white house with steeply pitched roof was as solid and sound as any house I had ever encountered. . . . It seemed very real. . . .

> . . . I wanted now to try something animate, something alive. I chose to try a mighty oak tree. It had to have a huge, thick trunk with large gnarled roots and countless branches in full leaf. Again, I repeated the same process as before, picturing in my mind each detail of the tree and then projecting that image forward to a particular spot to the right of the house, using my mind as a laser beam. . . . Presto, there was the tree complete with textured bark, insect holes, and vividly beautiful leaves.

> It happened! It was possible! It could be done! A human like myself could create from scratch. . . .

I was so overjoyed I went nuts.

*I went on a creation binge, bringing together, creating, form-
ing, and giving life to anything and everything I could imagine.
I made cities, people, dogs, cats, trash cans, alleys, telephone
poles, schools, books, pencils, cars, roads, lawns, birds, flowers,
shrubbery, rain, suns, clouds, rivers; and everything had life and
everything moved of its own and there was breath, noise, language and all manner of activity aside and apart from me. . . .
It was all so incredibly wonderful that I watched long and with
fascination . . . with a feeling of satisfaction that I had engaged in
an exercise perfectly normal for me to do and perfectly natural.
I rested.*

—Atwater, Coming Back to Life, 33–35.

A similar story comes from Nancy Danison. During her
NDE, Nancy observed that there was no tunnel. As soon as she
thought of a tunnel, one immediately formed. Then she tried
to will a green meadow, and immediately she was standing on
the grass. When she tried to imagine her hospital, she found
herself walking down its hallway. Video available at *nhne-nde
.org/resources/how-near-death-experiences-are-changing-the-world*,
19:16 to 21:50 (accessed August 14, 2013).

In this state, NDErs not only have access to creative power
but also to all knowledge. As P. M. H. Atwater describes it:

*. . . if I wanted to know what it was like to be the president of
the United States, I would need only to wish for the experience
and it would be so. Or if I wanted to know what it was like to
be an insect, I would merely have to "request" the experience by
wishing for it, and the experience would be mine.*

—Atwater, The Light Beyond, 43.

10. Jan Price, *The Other Side of Death*, 45–46; "Jan Price's Near-Death Experience with Her Pet Dog," 4.

11. Atwater, *Beyond the Light*, 13–14.

12. Sheridan, *Animals and the Afterlife*, 201–202.

13. Smith, *The Soul of Your Pet*, 40.

14. Atwater, *The New Children and Near-Death Experiences*, 110–111.

15. Lynn, *http://www.near-death.com/experiences/animals02.html* (accessed December 17, 2012).

Chapter 8: The Light

1. van Lommel, *Consciousness Beyond Life*, 2.

2. Pam Throgmorton, as recounted to Kathy McCabe. Personal correspondence January 6, 2015. Used with permission.

3. Moody, *Glimpses of Eternity*, 13–14.

4. Brian Bethune, "Why So Many People—Including Scientists—Suddenly Believe in an Afterlife: Heaven Is Hot Again, and Hell Is Colder than Ever," *MacLean's*, May 7, 2013, *http://www.macleans .ca/society/life/the-heaven-boom/* (accessed December 17, 2014).

5. Mellen-Thomas Benedict, *http://www.oneworldspirit.org/box14 .html* (accessed May 22, 2013).

6. Idem.

7. Moody, *Glimpses of Eternity*, 86.

8. "Kyle Crafton's NDE—'The Warmth Was Compassion,'" *https:// www.youtube.com/watch?v=lcOJoS6BXKw* (accessed May 31, 2015).

9. Moorjani, *Dying to Be Me*, 151, 167.

10. Atwater, *The New Children and Near-Death Experiences*, 109.

11. "Awake in the Dream: Mellen-Thomas Benedict About His Near-Death Experience," *https://www.youtube.com/watch?v= 8VQiVQ4fa_4* (accessed December 17, 2014).

12. Amy C., *http://www.nderf.org/NDERF/amy_c_nde_4720.html* (accessed December 16, 2014).

13. Atwater, *Coming Back to Life*, 100.

14. John Jay Harper, *Tranceformers: Shamans of the 21st Century* (Foresthill, CA: Reality Press, 2009), 147.

15. David Bohm, *Wholeness and the Implicate Order* (London: Routledge and Kegan Paul, 1980).

16. "Mellen-Thomas Benedict's Near-Death Experience," 14.

17. Moody, *The Light Beyond*, 137.

18. McTaggert, *The Bond*, 63–66; Gary E. Schwartz, *The Sacred Promise* (New York: Atria Books, 2011),193–194; "Expert Explores Theory of Reality and Near-Death Experience—Part I," *http://www*
.medindia.net/news/Interviews/expert-explores-theory-of-reality-and
-near-death-experience-part-i-111401-1.htm (accessed December 17, 2014).

19. "Mellen-Thomas Benedict's Near-Death Experience," 13.

20. See Dennis Linn, Sheila Fabricant Linn, and Matthew Linn, *Healing the Future: Personal Recovery from Societal Wounding*, which is about remembering who we are. It includes specific aspects of our culture that encourage us to forget, including competition, rewards and punishments, the often subtle emotional violence in much of our communication, and institutional structures based on domination (Mahwah, NJ: Paulist Press, 2012).

21. Ring, *Lessons from the Light*, 198.

Chapter 9: Affirming Love and Self-Esteem

1. "Oprah Winfrey Interviews Betty Eadie," *http://www.youtube.com*
/watch?v=6uUiYFaawTU (accessed March 17, 2014).

2. Sutherland, *Reborn in the Light*, 39.

3. Ibid., 138.

4. Idem.

5. van Lommel, *Consciousness Beyond Life*, 52. See also 46, 47, 53, 347.

6. "Ned Dougherty's Near-Death Experience and Visions of the Future," *http://near-death.com/dougherty.html* (accessed August 21, 2013).

7. "Near-Death Experience—Death Before Graduation," *https://www.youtube.com/watch?v=7sOSivLkYTA*

8. Moorjani, *Dying to Be Me*, 69–70.

Prologue to Chapters 9, 10, and 11: Life Review

1. William Joseph Bray, *Quantum Physics, Near Death Experiences, Eternal Consciousness, Religion, and the Human Soul* (Lexington, KY, 2011), 29.

2. Moody, *Glimpses of Eternity*, 10–12.

Chapter 10: Life Review: Memories of Love

1. "Understand the Gift to Enjoy the Treasure," *http://iands.org /experiences/nde-accounts/797-understand-the-gift-to-enjoy-the-treasure .html* (accessed August 5, 2012).

2. Long, *Evidence of the Afterlife*, 14.

3. Tijn Touber, "A New Lease on Life," interview with Pim van Lommel, 5.

4. *http://www.nderf.org/NDERF/NDE_Experiences/justin_u_nde.html* (accessed May 22, 2013).

5. Moody, *Glimpses of Eternity*, 14–15.

6. Erica McKenzie, "View with God's Glasses," *www.youtube.com /watch?v=xG_hEi8E4U8* (accessed December 18, 2014).

7. "Reinee Pasarow's Near-Death Experience," *http://near-death.com /forum/nde/000/64.html* (accessed December 18, 2014).

8. Kevin Williams, "Life Review and the Near-Death Experience," Introduction, *http://near-death.com/experiences/research24.html* (accessed December 18, 2014).

9. Kevin Williams, "Life Review and the Near-Death Experience," 10. Various Examples of Life Reviews, Thomas Sawyer's Life Review Insights, *http://near-death.com/experiences/research24.html* (accessed December 18, 2014).

10. Moody, *Glimpses of Eternity*, 95–97.

11. Betty Eadie, 10. Various Examples of Life Reviews, Betty Eadie's Life Review Experience, *http://near-death.com/experiences/research24 .html* (accessed December 18, 2014).

Chapter 11: Life Review: Who Has Hurt Me?

1. Ring, *Heading Toward Omega*, 105–106.

2. Ibid., 108.

3. Ibid., 109.

4. Ibid., 106

5. Idem.

6. *http://www.nderf.org/amy_c_nde4720.htm* (accessed December 16, 2014).

Chapter 12: Life Review: Whom Have I Hurt?

1. John Lerma, *Into the Light* (Pompton Plains, NJ: New Page Books, 2007), 95.

2. Ring, *Lessons from the Light*, 162.

3. Ibid., 175.

4. "Promo Video for Consciousness Continues: Surviving Death— Near Death Experience NDE," *http://www.youtube.com /watch?v=pgBdf1GqNIA* (accessed December 18, 2014).

5. "Rene Jorgensen—Bringing Light to Near-Death Experiences," Part 1, *https://www.youtube.com/watch?v=MNTgGQq78i8* (accessed January 23, 2015).

6. Betty Eadie, 10. Various Examples of Life Reviews, Betty Eadie's Life Review Experience, *http://near-death.com/experiences/research24.html* (accessed December 18, 2014).

7. David Lorimer, *Whole in One: The Near-Death Experience and the Ethic of Interconnectedness* (London: Arkana, 1990), 23, cited in Ring, *Lessons from the Light*, 160.

8. Berkley Carter Mills, *http://www.near-death.com/experiences/christianity09.html* (accessed December 20, 2014).

9. Atwater, *Coming Back to Life*, 36–37.

10. Ring, *Lessons from the Light*, 198.

11. Moody, *Glimpses of Eternity*, 180–182.

Chapter 13: Purpose: Why Am I (Still) Here?

1. BBC documentary, *The Day I Died*, 2002, *www.youtube.com/watch?v=R2JRHQ7E8w0* (accessed March 15, 2014).

2. Kersti Wistrand, "Swedish-Russian Research: Near Death Experiences and Other Transpersonal Experiences Among Women During Childbirth," Results, Case IV, *http://old.altstates.net/en/hbi/wistrand-swedish-russian-nde-2012* (accessed December 20, 2014).

3. Ring, *Lessons from the Light*, 151.

4. Present!—Barbara Whitfield's Near-Death Experience, *http://www.youtube.com/watch?v=rRCxZlv3Td8* (accessed December 20, 2014).

5. Jim Robbins, *The Man Who Planted Trees* (New York: Spiegel & Grau, 2012), 10.

6. Ibid., 106.

7. Ibid., 77.

8. Idem.

9. Ibid., inside front cover.

10. Idem.; "The Man Who Planted Trees—Pay It Forward to the Year 4012: David Milarch at TEDxSanJoseCA," *https://www.youtube.com/watch?v=XGMJT9H3Aok* (accessed March 31, 2015); "Cloning the World's Largest Trees to Help Minimize Global Warming," *https://www.youtube.com/watch?v=3qkEEjolpFU* (accessed March 31, 2015).

11. Michael Tymn, "An After-Death Visitation: Dr. Kubler-Ross Sees and Talks with Dead Woman," Source: Elisabeth Kubler-Ross, M.D., There Is No Death, *http://www.greaterreality.com/nodeath.htm* (accessed December 20, 2014).

12. Ring, *Lessons from the Light*, 47.

13. Ibid., 198.

14. Jan Price, *The Other Side of Death*, 51–53.

Chapter 14: The Examen: A Daily Life Review and a Way to Find Our Purpose

1. Ring, *Lessons from the Light*, 184.

2. "My Son, My Light," *http://iands.org/experiences/nde-accounts/939-my-son-my-light.html* (accessed September 1, 2013).

Chapter 15: Who Cares for Us from the Other Side?

1. Ring, *Lessons from the Light*, 50.

2. Anna W., *http://www.nderf.org/NDERF/NDE_Experiences/anna_w_nde_5426.htm* (accessed December 20, 2014).

3. Shelley Yates, "Fire the Grid," Part 1, *https://www.youtube.com/watch?v+TsxNW0i74x0*; Part 2, *https://www.youtube.com/watch?v=LGsMs2vj3WY*; Part 3, *https://www.youtube.com/watch?v=4A02qL1P3Jc* (accessed December 20, 2014).

4. Amy C., *http://www.nderf.org/NDERF/amy_c_nde_4720.htm* (accessed December 16, 2014).

5. Moorjani, *Dying to Be Me*, 66, 73–74.

6. Ibid., 66–67.

7. Alexander, *Proof of Heaven*, 95–96.

8. Bill and Judy Guggenheim, *Hello from Heaven!* (New York: Bantam, 1995), 193–194.

9. "Iranian Killer's Execution Halted at Last Minute by Victim's Parents," April 16, 2014, *Guardian*, *http://www.theguardian.com /world/2014/apr/16/iran-parents-halt-killer-execution* (accessed April 28, 2014).

10. Guggenheim, *Hello from Heaven!*, 367–368.

11. Personal communication, (November 2013)

Chapter 16: Love Heals the Body

1. Long, *Evidence of the Afterlife*, 130–131.

2. Kevin Williams, "Told Not Ready to Die and the Near-Death Experience," 2. Being Told "You're Not Ready to Die," *http://near -death.com/experiences/research31.html* (accessed December 20, 2014).

3. Long, *Evidence of the Afterlife*, 188.

4. Ring, *Heading Toward Omega*, 11–12.

5. Bernie Siegel, *Love, Medicine & Miracles* (New York: Harper, 1986), 181.

6. Moorjani, *Dying to Be Me*, 180.

7. Ibid., 138.

8. Ibid., 140.

9. Ibid., 145.

10. "Mellen-Thomas Benedict's Near-Death Experience," 5.

11. Ibid., 12.

12. Atwater, *Beyond the Light*, 130–131; Robert Blaich, *Your Inner Pharmacy: Taking Back Our Wellness* (Hillsboro, OR: Beyond Words Publishing, 2006).

13. C. W. F. McClare, "Resonance in Bioenergetics," *Annals of the New York Academy of Science* 227 (1974), 74–97. Cited in Bruce Lipton, *The Biology of Belief* (New York: Hay House, 2008), 81. Lipton writes that McClare's research "revealed that energetic signaling mechanisms such as electromagnetic frequencies are a hundred times more efficient in relaying environmental information than physical signals such as hormones, neurotransmitters, growth factors, etc."

14. Diarmuid O'Murchu, *Ancestral Grace: Meeting God in Our Human Story* (Maryknoll, NY: Orbis, 2008), 135.

15. *http://nhne-pulse.org/nde-powerful-quotes/* (accessed March 25, 2013).

16. Larry Dossey, *Healing Words: The Power of Prayer and the Practice of Medicine* (New York: Harper Collins, 1992), xviii, 205.

17. Quote regarding the efficacy of prayer and religious affiliation is from a letter from Dr. Larry Dossey to Dr. Martin Parmentier, December 3, 1994. Used with Dr. Dossey's permission.

18. P. M. H. Atwater, *We Live Forever: The Real Truth About Death* (Virginia Beach, VA: ARE Press, 2004), 131–132.

Chapter 17: Opening Ourselves to the Benign Virus

1. See Sheila Fabricant Linn, Dennis Linn, and Matthew Linn, *Healing Our Beginning* (Mahwah, NJ: Paulist Press, 2005).

2. Joan Fitzherbert, "The Source of Man's Intimations of Immortality," *British Journal of Psychiatry*, 110 (1964), 859–862.

3. William Joseph Bray, *Quantum Physics*, 226, #34.

4. Steven Raymond, "Cellular Consciousness and Conception: An Interview with Dr. Graham Farrant," *Pre- & Perinatal Psychology News*, II:2 (Summer, 1988), reprinted in *The Journal of Christian Healing*, 11:3 (Fall, 1989), 17–23.

5. Ring, *Lessons from the Light*, 198.

Chapter 18: Already Home: We Come from Where We Are Going

1. Alexander and Tompkins, *The Map of Heaven*, 91.

2. *The Prebirth Experience: Compelling Evidence of the Eternal Nature of Our Souls*, "I Told God No! from Debbie Redford," September 21, 2012, *http://sarahhinze.com/?p=560* (accessed December 21, 2014). For similar accounts of pre-birth experiences, see books by Sarah Hinze, e.g., *Coming from the Light: Spiritual Accounts of Life Before Life* (New York: Simon & Schuster, 1997). On pp. 176–178, Hinze compares the elements of a typical NDE with typical pre-birth experiences.

3. Sarah Hinze, *We Lived in Heaven: Spiritual Accounts of Souls Coming to Earth* (Provo, UT: Spring Creek Book Co., 2006).

4. *The Prebirth Experience*, op. cit.

Chapter 19: The Universal Donor

1. Kenneth Ring, personal correspondence, August 6, 2012.

2. Moody, *The Light Beyond*, 150.

3. Ring, *Heading Toward Omega*, 162–163, 316–317.

4. Ring, *Lessons from the Light*, 175.

5. Idem.

6. Moorjani, *Dying to Be Me*, 69, 75.

7. Kenneth Ring, personal correspondence.

8. David Sunfellow, "The Formula for Creating Heaven on Earth," *http://msv-nhne.org/the-formula-for-creating-heaven-on-earth/* (accessed December 21, 2014).

9. Atwater, *Near-Death Experiences*, 209. The study cited was done by the Pew Research Center's Forum on Religion and Public Life in 2009. It focuses on religious beliefs and practices that do not fit neatly into conventional categories.

10. Mellen-Thomas Benedict, *Coast to Coast* interview with George Noory, November 17, 2009.

11. Ring, *Lessons from the Light*, 162.

12. Ibid., 282.

Appendix A: Elements of a Near-Death Experience

1. Cited in van Lommel, *Consciousness Beyond Life*, 11–12.

Appendix B: Frequency of Near-Death Stages

1. Based on Long, *Evidence of the Afterlife*, *http://nhneneardeath.ning .com/forum/topics//book-summary-evidence-of-the-afterlife* (accessed September 1, 2013).

Appendix C: Life Changes After a Cardiac Arrest with and Without an NDE

1. van Lommel, *Consciousness Beyond Life*, 67, 69.

Additional Resources by the Linns

English Materials

For information about a booklet based on this book, titled *Accompanying a Loved One Home: Healing the Dying by Reflecting on Near-Death Experiences*, for use by those who are near death, their families and other loved ones, and caregivers, see the Linns' website, *www.linnministries.org*, or contact them at *info@ linnministries.org*.

The Linns have written twenty-three books, including *Sleeping with Bread: Holding What Gives You Life*, *Belonging: Bonds of Healing and Recovery*, and most recently *Healing the Future: Personal Recovery from Societal Wounding*. Their books for children include *What Is My Song?* and *Making Heart-Bread*. All of the Linns' books and audiovisual materials and how to obtain them are listed on their website, *www.linnministries.org*.

Spanish Materials

All of the Linns' books and most of their audiovisual materials are available in Spanish. For more information, see their website, *www.linnministries.org*.

Retreats, Seminars, and Conferences

For information about retreats, seminars, and conferences in English and Spanish by the authors, please contact them at (970) 476-9235, *info@linnministries.org*, or see their website, *www.linnministries.org*.

About the Authors

Sheila, John, and Denny

Matt

Dennis, Sheila, and Matt Linn work together as a team, integrating physical, emotional and spiritual wholeness. They have taught courses on processes for healing in over sixty countries and in many universities and hospitals, including a course to doctors accredited by the American Medical Association. They are the authors of twenty-three books, including two books for children and those who care for them. These books have sold over a million copies in English and have been translated into more than twenty languages. Dennis and Sheila live in Colorado with their son, John. Matt lives in a Jesuit community in Minnesota.

Hampton Roads Publishing Company
. . . for the evolving human spirit

Hampton Roads Publishing Company
publishes books on a variety of subjects, including
spirituality, health, and other related topics.

For a copy of our latest trade catalog,
call (978) 465-0504 or visit our distributor's website at
www.redwheelweiser.com.

You can also sign up for our newsletter and special
offers by going to *www.redwheelweiser.com/newsletter/.*